The Dust Bowl:
Living in Tough Times

CLEO LAMPOS

The Dust Bowl, Living in Tough Times, First Edition

Text copyright © Cleo Lampos, Chi-Town Books, 2017 All Rights Reserved

Cover design by designwit on fiveer

All scripture quotations are taken from The Holy Bible, NIV. All Rights Reserved.

All rights reserved. No part of this publication may be reproduced, stored in a retrieval system, or transmitted in any form or by any means—electronic, mechanical, photocopying, recording, or otherwise—without the prior written permission of the author. The only exception is brief quotations in printed reviews.

References to real people, events, establishments, organizations, or locales are intended only to provide authenticity.

ISBN-13: 978-1979321679
ISBN-10: 1979321671

DEDICATION

To my mother, Ina, and my father, Jesse

My parents were married in 1930 and lived on the cusp of the Dust Bowl with my brother, Wilbur. Their perseverance in the face of adversity has provided a precious legacy. Reading a decade of Great Depression era letters, as well as my mother's diaries, revealed a story far more intense than fiction.

And to Sherri Wilson Johnson who has worked diligently with her skills to present the history of the Dust Bowl.

CONTENTS

INTRODUCTION i
Chapter One 1
Chapter Two 4
Chapter Three 9
Chapter Four 14
Chapter Five 19
Chapter Six 23
Chapter Seven 27
Chapter Eight 32
Chapter Nine 37
Chapter Ten 43
Chapter Eleven 48
Chapter Twelve 53
Chapter Thirteen 57
Chapter Fourteen 61
Chapter Fifteen 65
Chapter Sixteen 69
Chapter Seventeen 74
Chapter Eighteen 78
Chapter Nineteen 83
Chapter Twenty 90
Chapter Twenty-One 93
Chapter Twenty-Two 97
Chapter Twenty-Three 103
Chapter Twenty-Four 109
Chapter Twenty-Five 114
Conclusion 119
Photo Credits and Links 121

INTRODUCTION

"How can you frighten a man whose hunger is not only in his own cramped stomach but in the wretched bellies of his children? You can't scare him- he has known a fear beyond every other."

From **Grapes of Wrath,** by John Steinbeck

How does one live in difficult circumstances?
How does the depravity of youth affect the productivity of adulthood?
How does a mother feed her children in a world of swirling dust?
How does a farmer plant a crop in a drought with roiling Black Blizzards scraping off the top soil?
How can a person find relief from a parched soul?
The following essays invite the reader into the world of the Dust Bowl.
To a decade where perseverance and hope kept ranchers scratching on piles of dirt.
It is an opportunity to learn from history the key to surviving in the midst of difficulties.

"You gain strength, courage and confidence by every experience in which you really stop to look fear in the face. You are able to say to yourself, 'I lived through this horror. I can take the next thing that comes along. You must do the things you think you cannot do." –
Eleanor Roosevelt.

Chapter One
The Dust Bowl: How Did It Happen?

Childhood memories

Living in Greeley, Colorado, as a child, water conservation made perfect sense. My mother used a wringer washing machine with two tubs of rinse water. After hanging the wet clothes on the lines, she emptied the tubs by carrying buckets of the water to the strawberry bed, the potato patch and the pea vines climbing on strings alongside the house. Not a drop was wasted. Not a blade of grass grew in the back yard. Only in the front, where it held down a small patch of dirt. The back yard yielded to my old spoons and other utensils as I made mud pies and built roads in the sandy soil. When dusty winds kicked up, I knew to pull a kerchief over my nose and mouth to prevent suffocation. My life as a youngster in mid-century drew from hard earned knowledge carved by the Black Blizzards of the 1930's.

Epicenter of the Dust Bowl

Greeley is a city on the cusp of the Dust Bowl. The primary impact of the devastating Black Blizzards was on the southern plains of Kansas, the Oklahoma Panhandle, northern Texas, and western Colorado. The effects of the dust storms ranged all across the Great Plains from New Mexico to the Dakotas. The area suffered for a decade from the yellowish-brown haze from the South to the rolling walls of black dust from the North. The drought and windblown dust created agricultural decline which buried the farmers and ranchers in mounds of debt. That resulted in bank foreclosures. Those who stayed on the semi-arid land hung onto their sanity and homesteads with scraping fingernails.

Warnings Unheeded

The Dust Bowl should never have happened. The Native Peoples warned the suitcase farmers not to plow the earth. The old-time cattle ranchers talked about native grasses' holding the soil. But the lure of easy money drove easterners to invest in tearing up the sod to plant wheat. Their poor agricultural practices and years of sustained drought predicted by the Native Peoples caused the Dust Bowl. The ground that held the soil in place had been plowed up. There was nothing to stop the plains' winds from whipping across the fields and rising in dark roiling clouds of dust. The skies darkened for days at a time. Year after year. Even sealed houses had thick layers of dust on everything. Electrical shocks were produced by the dust on metal. Cows suffocated in the storms. Grown men lost all hope, women stared with dry eyes at the sand piles covering their chicken coops. Some succumbed to despair. All that flourished were the unrelenting dust, the swarms of jackrabbits, tumbleweeds and desperation.

The Cost of Greed

Greed. That is the bottom line to why the dust bowl emerged. Those who had lived on the land, learned the rhythms of the rain, and respected the nature around them warned the big investors of the consequences of their money motivated actions. As an adult, looking back at the period of time in the 1930 to 1939, it is not surprising why mankind ended up in a mess. The question became just one: how to get out of it and reclaim the creation.

In the time of deepest need, musicians pour out their hearts in a way to bring comfort to the distressed. Thomas Mosie Lister wrote a song, **"*Til the Storm Passes By*"**. *Imagine sitting in a Black Blizzard where you cannot see your hand in front* of your face. Read the lyrics from an online source, and feel God's arms wrap around you.

Chapter Two
Henry Finnell: The Dust Storm's Answer to "If it rain"

"The Black Blizzards were fearful. A giant wall rolling toward you like a steamroller." – Floyd Coen

Learning to Live in the Desert

Growing up in Oklahoma Territory in the early 1900's, Henry Finnell learned the ways of the semi-arid land on his parents' homestead. He graduated from the local high school in Stillwater, then earned an agronomy and erosion degree from the Oklahoma Agricultural and Mechanical College in 1917. Armed with a green thumb, Finnell became foreman of the Panhandle Experiment Station. For this gangly youth, it was his dream job. During the next seventeen years, he watched the crops fail in the Panhandle. He devised ways to utilize water more efficiently in the dry soil and pioneered methods to combat the loss of the topsoil to erosion. Methodically, he wrote reports and published articles, but his findings were ignored by the agriculture community.

Until the devastating prolonged drought of the 1930's.

Dust Bowl farm, Coldwater District, Texas Photo by Dorothea Lange, Courtesy of Library of Congress

The Farmers Hope: "If it rains"

Hugh Bennett, head of the Soil Conservation Service, approached the Oklahoma soil expert whose publications had caught his eye years before. Bennett presented Finnell with the challenge of a lifetime. Live in Dalhart, the epicenter of the agricultural misery of Region Six. This area defined the drought stricken Great Plains. The code name for Finnell's work, Operation Dustbowl, said it all. Finnell accepted the overwhelming responsibility. He worked in spite of dust storms which pounded the region, blotting out the sun for hours, piling dust hills that covered sheds, killing animals and human beings with dust pneumonia, and preventing vegetation from growing. He began by talking with any farmers who would listen to him. These suspicious workers of the land balked at Finnell's ideas, even as the banks foreclosed on one after another acreage. Eventually the phrase, "if it rains" evaporated like a drop of water in the prairie sun as hope for recovery dwindled.

Photo from Wikimedia Commons

The Dust Bowl Whisperer

The men from the CCC Civilian Conservation Corps brought their tents to the region, and Finnell set them to work. Under Finnell's direction, they developed thirteen demonstration projects to show farmers the new techniques that saved topsoil and water. Finnell determined which acres to turn into grassland and the CCC bulldozed the high sand dunes into flat ground. After assessing wind erosion, Finnell made a plan and the WPA Works Project Administration planted 220 million trees to create a windbreak that stretched 18,600 miles from Oklahoma to Canada. With examples by Finnell, the farmers learned to contour plow, terrace, use list plows and strip plant. Finnell showed how to capture dampness into the soil through moisture conservation. By 1938, farmers cashed in on crops where a marginal amount of rain fell. They soaked in Finnell's advice like cool showers on parched earth. Finnell led the way to slow improvement as people regained their soul, their soil, and their lives.

For Such a Time

A kid growing up in Oklahoma Territory loving to work with soil. Experimenting with dirt. Researching farming techniques. A vehicle from which and through which deliverance for a people was given. Henry Finnell. Born for such a time as this.

During the 1930's, a young Chicago musician, Thomas A. Dorsey, wrote blues songs, then gospel music. His splintered life finally took a turn for happiness when his wife became pregnant. With the sudden death of his wife and new born son, grief overcame him. The Dust Bowl farmers recognized his raw emotions expressed in a blues infused song that he composed. Find the words to <u>PRECIOUS LORD, TAKE MY HAND</u>, *and hear the cry of the farmers of the 1930s blend with Dorsey's impassioned plea.*

For an informative video on Finnell, check this out on PBS:

http://www.pbs.org/kenburns/dustbowl/bios/henry-howard-finnell and for some great photos, click here: http://www.pbs.org/kenburns/dustbowl/photos

Chapter Three
Hugh Hammond Bennett
The Dust Bowl's Advocate

Who grows up wanting to be a soil surveyor? What is a soil surveyor, anyway? Hugh Bennett, that's who. A man who classifies soil types and decides the vegetation and land use patterns for certain areas of land. The exact person needed during the 1930's in the Great Plains as topsoil blew away by the ton.

A Boy and His Dirt

In 1881, Hugh Hammond Bennett was born in North Carolina on his father's cotton farm. The agriculture practice of planting tobacco or cotton every year for decades had depleted the soil and decreased profits. Hugh roamed his family's acreage, observing the soil erosion year after year but not hearing any explanations about prevention. Bennett graduated from the University of North Carolina in 1902 as a soil surveyor and found a job in the United States Government. This allowed him to travel to other countries where he studied soil. He learned the differences between marginal rainfall and crop production. He learned how tropical humidity effected plants. He noticed the woods, forests, pastures, wildlife and the interconnections between them. Excited about his newfound knowledge, he wrote publications, but received little public response.

The Southwest

As Bennett served in the Southwest in the late 1920's, he decided soil erosion was becoming a crisis. The farmers laughed at him when he decried their straight row planting on land with marginal rainfall. Then the rains stopped. Crops failed. Worse, the topsoil rose from the ground in vast dust storms, stripping the land of fertile ground. President Roosevelt appointed Bennett as head of the Soil Erosion Service in 1933. His job: teach the farmers new agricultural techniques. The farmers balked. The Great Plains threatened to become the new Sahara Desert.

Dynamic Duo of the Dust

Bennett needed help, and he knew the right person. A young man who caught his attention. A conservationist like himself who had also published articles about soil erosion. An agronomist who worked quietly with pioneering methods to combat the loss of Oklahoma topsoil. Bennett contacted Henry Finnell and offered him the job of living in the epicenter of the drought. Bennet sighed in relief as the quiet Finnell set up shop in Region Six, Operation Dustbowl. He gave him full authority to create demonstration farms, plant shelterbelts and bulldoze piles of dust. Together, Finnell and Bennett visited hundreds of farmers and talked to them about how to work the land in a different way. In 1935, just as they made a sliver of progress, the funding dried up like the plains surrounding them. Congress needed the money for the Great Depression out East. Who cared if a few grain farmers went under?

Bennett and the D.C. Storm

As head of Soil Conservation Service, Bennett was called to Washington, DC to defend his work before a Congressional subcommittee. Knowing he left his work in the capable hands of Finnell, he traveled to the nation's capital. Having lived for years in the midst of swirling dust storms, his internal radar blipped on. He went with his instincts and arrived at the Congress on the appointed day, March 21. Bennett had the floor and every ear of the Congress. The air around Bennett bristled from anticipation as well as barometric changes. Familiar, but subtle, dynamics that coincided with a huge dust storm that had kicked up in the Midwest and roiled east. Bennett explained with charts and statistics for hours about how the bill, HR 7054, would stop the blowing away of America's topsoil. The nodding heads and yawning Congressmen signaled boredom, but Bennett knew the signs of the Black Blizzards, so he droned on. Soon the sky grew overcast. Light in Congress dimmed. Everyone stared at the windows as a dust storm rolled over the building. Thick black clouds. Air heavy with grit that irritated the dignitaries' throats and noses. Darkness.

In a dramatic gesture, Bennett raised his hand and sighed. "Gentlemen. This is what I have been talking about." The bill passed. Less than a month later, April 14, 1935, the Dust Bowl experienced the most frightening dust storm ever on what was dubbed, "Black Sunday."

Picture by Arthur Rothenstein for the WPA National Archives

Two men who loved to learn about nature as children team

up as soil surveyors to reverse the greatest man-made natural disaster on this continent: Hugh Bennett and Henry Finnell.

Black Sunday brought the most frightening of all the Black Blizzards. Among those who huddled in shelters was a 22-year-old songwriter in a small house in Texas just south of No Man's Land. He described the event. "We watched the dust storm come up, like the Red Sea closing in on the Israel children. We sat in a little room and you couldn't see your hand before your face. People said, 'This is the end of the world.' Everyone replied, 'So long, it's been good to know you.'" Woody Guthrie wrote his iconic song, **So Long, It's Been Good to Know You.** *As poverty-stricken people migrated to California, this is the tune that others sang to send them on their way. Read the words of the song and imagine sitting at a table in complete darkness during the day.*

Chapter Four
Feed Sacks: The Fabric of the Dust Bowl

My inheritance from my mother lay in a large grocery bag filled with twelve-inch muslin squares cut from feed bags. A transfer depicting each one of the 48 state birds and flowers lay with every white square. With a bit of tenacity, I started embroidering those designs collected in the 1930's Dust Bowl. After completing ten of them, life intervened, and the project sat in my back closet for thirty years.

Creativity from a Sack

In the 1930's, feed sacks became the life line for housewives who needed to provide food and clothing for their families in a time of deprivation. The answer to their frugal living arrived in the plain white flour and sugar bags as well as the grain sacks used for livestock. The first designs on flour sacks by the George P. Plant Milling Company of St. Louis, Missouri featured gingham plaids with big or little checks in a variety of colors.

Picture of girls in feed sack clothing taken by Dorthea Lange, WPA Project Archives

The checked patterns worked well for the aprons that housewives wore over dresses to protect from dirt and food splatters as well as to wipe noses, remove pans from the oven, and swat flies. With the introduction of calicos, the colorful feed bags enticed women to go to the country stores with their husbands to pick out the large sacks that held the prettiest patterns. Now, the livestock could be fed and the family dressed in new shirts, dresses and skirt. Artists designed the fabrics in rich tones that added only five cents to the cost of a bag of feed. A bargain in those days.

Adding a Personal Touch

With creativity, a housewife's ability to add charm to her home became possible. A little rickrack. A crocheted collar. Embroidered designs. Smocking. A needle and thread allowed a bit of fabric to become beauty in the midst of difficulty. By the middle of the 1930's, over 3 million women, including Elenore Roosevelt herself, wore dress sack creations. Women organized Sack and Swap parties to trade dress-print bags. Some women exchanged remnants from their home projects to coordinate colors needed to stitch a quilt.

Warmth of Home

With the wisdom of youth, Dennis McCann observed, "Those must have been depressing times, those long-ago days of bread and milk, of feedbag clothes and canned weed dinners. Of little or nothing." Jane Tamse countered in her feeble, quivering voice. "Those were frugal days, but they left us with a happy childhood."

Finishing the Quilt

After thirty years, I rediscovered the bag of my mother's feed sack squares at age 63, just when my granddaughter, Ramona, turned 16. We took the project to a quilting guild. We went once a month for a year to finish stitching the quilt, using period piece fabric for the finishing touches. Now, Ramona sleeps in college under a quilt that she stitched. Its layers are packed with love from her great-grandmother and her grandmother, who finally embroidered enough squares for a twin sized comforter. A cozy reminder of the strong women in our family from the 1930's until now.

Ramona Clark and Cleo Lampos with finished quilt started by Cleo's mother in the Dust Bowl with feed sack muslin squares and transfers from newspapers.

"Stitch together scraps of family love into a warm memory quilt that cradles in its folds encouragement and truth that still apply."- Anonymous

Chapter Five
Hobos - The Dust Bowl's Rail Riders

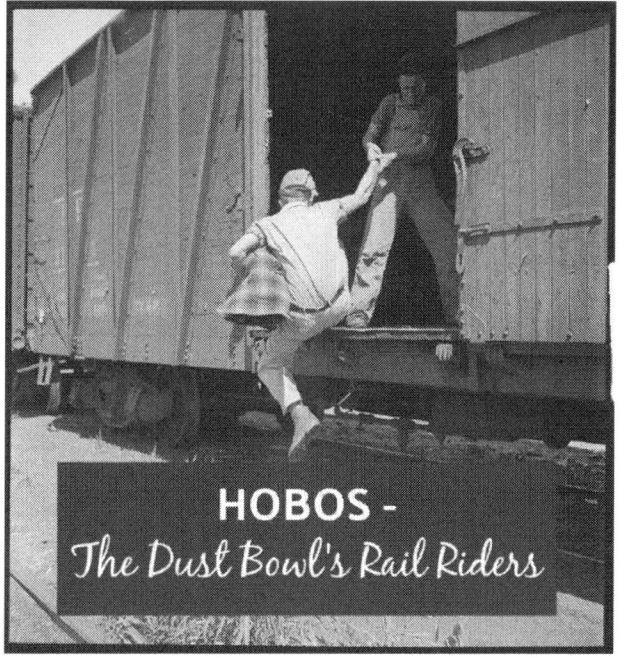

Hobos. Not bums. Not tramps. Hobos.

A 17-year-old kid like Gene Wadsworth who caught his first freight train on a winter's night in 1932. The pain of being orphaned at age 11 followed him to his uncle's house in Idaho where five other children needed feeding. Like many of the two million plus hobos, Gene joined those men traveling the country, seeking daily jobs that promised a meal.

Hobo hopping a freight train in 1935

Or an 18-year-old graduate of high school who tearfully left his family in Duluth because he realized the burden he added to the daily scrounging for food. Leslie E. Paul became a man at a young age.

The same story drove Henry Kuezur to leave his East Chicago home in 1932. One less mouth to feed in a family of eight children. His unemployed father supplied only enough for potato soup at each meal. Henry heard of work in California where nobody starved, and took to the rails.

As unemployment skyrocketed in the Great Depression, husbands left families with relatives in a search for work. Some found employment and sent back some money. Others didn't. But most rode the trains as hobos: those who hoped someday to be **Ho**meward **Bo**und.

Hobos searching for work

Hobo life proved to be dangerous. Jumping onto a train meant accidents. If caught trying to hop a ride on a freight, a hobo faced a night in jail or a beating by the club wielding railroad yard men. Over 6,500 hoboes were killed in one year by misfortune or railroad guards. Starvation, disease and despair trailed after each hobo like burrs on a dog's tail.

Hobos sought work. Tramps only worked if forced by police. Bums never worked. Every hobo had a trade: shoe repair, making wire fruit bowls, hoeing a garden, playing music. They tried to make spare change by furnishing a service like chopping wood. Many found migratory worker jobs that paid per diem, but necessitated moving on.

The center of hobo life was the camp located near the railroads and a water supply. There were strict rules imposed on those who gathered around the campfires.

Older men protected the teens from predators. They shared food, advice, and memories with each other, and helped the vulnerable. Camp justice proved to be a reason to behave in a civil manner.

Although no real names were used by hobos, nicknames identified features of their lives. Oklahoma Slim, Box Car Willie, North Bank Fred. Some men who later became household names found themselves in the hobo jungles. Louis L'Amour, Jack London, Jack Kerouac, Art Linkletter, Eric Sevareid, Jack Dempsy, Carol Sandburg, and Woody Guthrie. The journey to a paying job led many of these men onto paths of compassion and determination.

Hobos put life into sharp perspective. Life was fleeting. It could pull up short on anybody. The people of the Dust Bowl lived with uncertainty, and had to hunker together to survive. On their train rides, these men longed for only one thing: better times that would propel them home. **Ho**meward **Bo**und. A hobo.

Woody Guthrie, famous for his gritty Oklahoma style guitar music, traveled on the hobo express from town to town before making his way to California. As a result of singing in hobo camps, seeing the opportunities and challenges of the Great Depression up close, he wrote a song that we love today. "THIS LAND IS MY LAND".

Chapter Six
Hoovervilles: The Cities of the Great Depression

I grew up knowing about Hoovervilles because my mother made a point of telling me about them. My mother and father were married in 1930. They moved to the Great Plains where my father dug irrigation ditches and spud cellars with a dragline. A wooden trailer that hitched behind their truck became their moveable home. Everything they owned fit into what my mother dubbed "Our bungalow of dreams." In a voice filled with emotion, she described the

Hooverville near the Rocky Mountains where people lived in tents or makeshift shacks. Then she added: "Your father had a job. We had food and a place to stay." My mother's appreciation for humble living has affected my own journey in life by helping me to understand the old adage, "There, but for the grace of God, am I."

Hoovervilles resulted from the massive foreclosures on families who lost their jobs and then their homes. Renters fell behind and were evicted. Relatives became overwhelmed by the number of people needing a place to live. Some families found vacant buildings to live in. Others sheltered under bridges, in culverts, empty water mains, or on unused public land.

Shanty towns built by homeless families bore the name of President Hoover, who was in office at the start of the Great Depression: Hoovervilles. The shelters consisted of anything that could be found, and reflected the carpenter skills of the maker. Wooden crates, cardboard, tar paper, metal scraps, stones, and bricks served as construction material. Most occupants owned a small stove, a few pots and pans, some bedding and little else. Hoovervilles tended to be located near a water source and a soup kitchen. Many planted vegetable gardens to supplement their food intake. The adults tried to find seasonal work. There was little help from any agency.

No one knows how many hundreds of thousands of people lived in these settlements. But with 25% of the workforce, or 13 million people, out of work, it is probable that a great number of displaced families spent some time in Hoovervilles before they got back onto their feet. The residents of these makeshift cities had nowhere else to go.

Public sentiments favored them, because, like my mother, everyone lived one pay check from homelessness. Even when they were torn down for unsanitary reasons, the men who carried out the government's orders often expressed regret and guilt for their actions. Maybe because they knew the people who lived there were from the old neighborhood, or were relatives.

When I reached adulthood, mother gave me a felt pin decorated with tiny beads, stitched by a woman in a Colorado Hooverville. When I take it out of the box and look at the amazing skill used to make it, an overpowering emotion floods through me. Appreciation. For the lessons of the Dust Bowl, and for the blessings of my parents' legacy.

Dorethea Lange photo from WPA archives

One of inspiring aspects of Hooverville was the music that the occupants gathered to create and enjoy. Many were musicians with violins, fiddles, guitars, and percussion instruments like scrub boards. They sang songs of unrequited love like "The Red River Valley." They may have dreamt with Dorothy as they crooned, "Somewhere Over the Rainbow." But, the songs of Gene Autry and Roy Rogers gathered all their voices. "You Are My Sunshine" and "Happy Trails to You." The healing of music to the spirit in the times of difficulty helped these people to make it to the better days.

Chapter Seven
Dust Pneumonia: When Breathing is Deadly

Dust Pneumonia

Dust pneumonia. A respiratory illness that slithered like a snake across the Texas Panhandle, Oklahoma, and Colorado during the 1930's. The continual coughing jag, high fever, nausea, chest pains and shortness of breath signaled the dreaded condition. Old people succumbed. Those afflicted with bronchitis, asthma or tuberculosis breathed in the dust to their detriment. But dust pneumonia attacked the infants and young children without mercy. At least 500 persons suffocated on the fine dust in the Dust Bowl.

A Permeating Dust

Dust everywhere. The tiniest particles floated in the air, making every breath closer to clogging the lungs with "gunk". Many coughed up mud, trying to clear their passages from the ever-present dirt. The mucous membranes were irritated in much the same manner as miners who had worked underground all their lives. The animals and livestock died from lungs packed with the dirt. There seemed no escape from the deadly menace.

Library of Congress Photo

No Escape

There was no way to keep the dirt out of a house, even with towels covering window openings. Caroline Henderson described her home. "Dust to eat and dust to breathe and dust to drink. Dust in the beds and in the flour bin, on dishes and walls and windows, in hair and eyes and ears and teeth and throats, to say nothing of the heaped-up accumulation on floors and windowsills. This wind-driven dust, fine as the finest flour, penetrates wherever air can go."

Photo by WPA and Red Cross

Masks in School

The Red Cross distributed over 10,000 masks for families to wear. The students in one room school houses sat in their desks breathing through masks that filtered the dusty air. Pauline Arnett Hodges remembers, "It was scary to me as a child, but it was better than choking." The Red Cross declared a medical emergency around the epicenter of the Dust Bowl. Makeshift hospital wards were opened in churches and high school auditoriums. A doctor in Oklahoma treated 56 patients, including a farmhand. He looked down the seventeen-year-old's throat and declared, "Young man, you are filled with dirt." The teen died three days later. Parents packed up their children and begged relatives in neighboring states to care for these little ones.

Moving to less dusty air saved the lives of many youngsters.

"Do the thing that you think you cannot do"

Eleanor Roosevelt, wife of President Roosevelt, expressed great compassion for the women of the Dust Bowl and Great Depression. She acknowledged their suffering and their fear. **"You gain strength, courage and confidence by every experience in which you really stop to look fear in the face. You are able to say to yourself, 'I have lived through this horror. I can take the next thing that comes along. You must do the thing that you think you cannot do."**

Like many of us, Eleanor Roosevelt stood by the casket of a baby or young child and grieved with the parents at this unimaginable loss. Like us, her tears ran unchecked and watered the dirt at her feet. But this wife of the president meant her words not just for those who had lost their child. She spoke to the parents who comforted their youngsters in the darkness of the Black Blizzards, and nursed them back to health when dust pneumonia threatened to take them. To the people of the Dust Bowl: **"You must do the thing that you think you cannot do."**

Library of Congress Photo

During the 1930's, one of the songs played at funerals was "Whispering Hope." Septimus Winner based this hymn on Hebrews 6:19. "Which hope we have as an anchor of the soul, both sure and steadfast, and which entereth into that within the veil."

This song has comforting words: "Wait till the darkness is over, wait till the tempest is done, Hope for the sunshine tomorrow, After the shower is gone. Whispering hope."

Quotes in this article come from the book, **The Dust Bowl**, by Dayton Duncan and Ken Burns.

Chapter Eight
The Dust Bowl Diet: Eating in a Drought

The Dust Bowl Diet:
Eating in a Drought

"How can you frighten a man whose hunger is not only in his own cramped stomach but in the wretched bellies of his children? You can't scare him--he has known a fear beyond every other."

John Steinbeck, *Grapes of Wrath*

Sunshine in a Jar

Having been raised in farming country by a frugal mother, late summer meant only one thing: canning. Our home lacked air conditioning, so she saved the canning for evenings. Think of the "dog days" of August and a lug of peaches. My job involved washing the jars and checking rims for cracks or chips. Sometimes I was promoted to peeling the peaches or sliding the skins off tomatoes or beets. The rest, my mother and sister completed. Dripping in sweat, we did not leave the kitchen until it was spic and span, which meant that the moon shone brightly and the stars twinkled to the cricket and frog concert. Since my first year of marriage, I have been canning. My husband admires the effort and calls it **"Sunshine in a jar."**

It is easy for me to romanticize the canning process, but to those in the Dust Bowl, food preservation meant life or death to a family. In the epicenter of the drought, not a blade of grass grew in the dirt. Farmers on the cusp of the area tended gardens with straggly dried up plants. If the heat and lack of water didn't kill their vegetation, then the

Black Blizzards, rabbit swarms and grasshopper plagues finished the job.

Tumbling Tumbleweeds

Rita Van Amber recalls. "Paying for a farm during the depression would serve as a hard task master for the very hardiest. My mother used to tell me that one of the lowest points was when she had to can weeds. The garden didn't do well, but the weeds, lamb's quarters and tumbleweeds still flourished. So she canned them, for something to put on the cellar shelves against the winter. Yet, my mother was such an innovative cook that to this day I still love those greens." The story of canned tumbleweed leaves is a familiar one in the personal accounts of those who lived during the 1930's.

Compassionate Canning

The Ball Canning Corporation set up public projects to help people in depressed areas. They created community canning operations to teach safe canning and provide equipment for backyard or farm gardens. Eventually, 3,800 community canning kitchens serviced struggling families with equipment for canning for a meager fee. For cash strapped housewives with no pressure canners, this proved to be a life saver.

Suppertime in the Dust Bowl

The standard meal at the table of those in the Dust Bowl consisted of "Jack, biscuits, and beans." The area was overrun with hordes of rabbits. Flour for biscuits proved affordable, and, well, beans are always a choice for fiber and sustenance. In the spring, a dandelion salad tasted mighty good.

WPA picture from National Archives

Supper time meant fried potato peel sandwiches, hard boiled eggs in white sauce over rice, toast soaked in milk gravy, popcorn with milk, oatmeal, cornbread, or a casserole made from a "little of this and a little of that." No one dared to complain, because the menu depended on what could be scrounged for the day. The mothers cooked meals made of nothing to try to fill the stomachs of their families. These were a proud people who didn't want to admit that times were hard in their place, no matter how tough it got. This taught the children to dig deep to find the best in themselves, to succeed, to perform. Life was either sink or swim, and nobody was going to drown on these parents' watch.

Looking at the shelves full of colorful jars of veggies from this year's urban homestead's harvest, my heart swells with appreciation for the legacy of those in the Dust Bowl and lessons they taught me about frugal living.

*One of the songs made famous by radio and cowboys was "****You Are My Sunshine****". Singing that song around the kitchen lifted the spirits of everyone in the family. Sunshine in the people. Sunshine in the jars of preserved food.*

*The **Sons of the Pioneers** strummed their guitars and crooned about "**Tumbling Tumbleweeds.**" Knowing that the housewives of that time were canning the leaves of these plants gives a different slant to that song.*

One of the chapters in the book, **Dust Between the Stitches**, describes how the main characters process a bushel of apples in a community canning center.

Stories and Recipes of the Great Depression of the 1930's -- *This book (pictured to the right) is packed with personal anecdotes about the Great Depression as well as some basic recipes..*

Chapter Nine
Leo Hart: The School for Dust Bowl Refugees

**Leo Hart:
The School for Dust Bowl Refugees**

"The people in flight from the terror behind had strange things happen to them: some bitterly cruel and some so beautiful that their faith is refired forever." - John Steinbeck, *Grapes of Wrath*

Leo Hart refired faith.

Maybe Leo Hart, Superintendent of Kern County Schools in the 1930's, developed his own faith growing up in rural

God-fearing Iowa with a school teacher mother and hard-working father. Maybe his convictions grew as he fought in France during World War I, then battled tuberculosis in a sanitarium. With his new-found health, he earned a master's degree in education, taught in Bakerfield's high school, then became superintendent of schools. Right in the district where John Steinbeck lived, worked and wrote his novel about the Oakie immigrants. People who left the Oklahoma Dust Bowl with all their earthly possessions in rattle-trap cars to work as migrant laborers for starvation wages in California. Leo Hart's faith led him to reach out to the disheveled children living in the tents of Weedpatch Camp with belief in the potential of these ragtag waifs.

Taxpayers and Teachers

Contrast Hart's faith in these Oakie refugees with the cynicism of the taxpayers in Kern County. The community regarded the newcomers as "uneducable" and their baggy overalls and tattered dresses as offensive to civilized standards. The teachers moved the migrant worker's kids to the back of the room because their unwashed bodies smelled. The biscuits they brought for lunch caused gagging noises from the local students. Unkempt hair, incomplete knowledge of the alphabet, and lack of school supplies led to both staff and classmates ignoring the Oakies. The humiliated ragamuffins fought back, their spicy language and tight fists flying to their defense.

Families from Oklahoma's Dust Bowl traveled to California with the hope of jobs. FSA Photo

The Call of Faith

Hart analyzed the problem. "I needed to find out what to do for these children to get them adjusted into society and take their rightful places." Watching the dust bowl survivors on the playground, in classrooms and in their camp, Hart realized the effect of years of deprivation on these children's lives. But he also viewed them as "ordinary boys and girls with the same hopes and dreams as the rest of us have." With deep faith in the ability of pupils to respond to caring, consistent teaching, Hart began an experiment in building a new kind of school: The Arvin Federal Emergency School. A place for the displaced Dust Bowl kids that would not be associated with the school district. No funding needing. The taxpayers applauded. On the site next to the migrant workers' camp, Hart started the school with no grass, no sidewalks, no playground equipment, no toilets, no water, no books, no teachers. Just two condemned buildings and "50 poorly clad, undernourished and skeptical youngsters."

And Leo Hart.

The School of Hard Times

The rest is history. Hart set out to provide the unwanted children "with educational experiences in a broader and richer curriculum than were present in most schools." During the summer of 1940, he interviewed teachers who wanted an adventure. Then he became a panhandler: a beggar of wood, scrounger of nails, borrower of books and paper. From the National Youth Authority, he received 25,000 bricks, from Sears Roebuck, an assortment of sheep, pigs and cows, from local nurseries, plants and vegetables, from ranchers, farm machinery. In September, Hart met with the faculty and students on a barren stretch of land piled high with bricks, boards, crates and boxes. They all went to work, and brick by brick built the school. The students laid pipe for water. The teachers taught how to make desks from orange crates. In the traditions of George Washington Carver and Booker T. Washington, the adults helped the children learn life-giving skills. To extend the curriculum further, a local butcher demonstrated meat cutting, and volunteer cooks helped the home economics class to use the produce that they grew in the gardens. An old boxcar was moved to the school and the boys learned to plaster, add plumbing and wiring. The school became self-sufficient with livestock and gardens, increasing the nutritional intake of the students. An incentive to attain high grades was the promise to drive the airplane up and down the runway. Soon, truancy and behavior problems disappeared. Hart claimed, "We left everything lying around and no one ever stole a thing."

Kern Migrants Camp. Photograph by Dorothea Lange. (Library of Congress)

A Living Legacy

Leo Hart's personal convictions led him to see potential where others only viewed problems. The children of the *Grapes of Wrath* who attended a school that they made with their own hands grew up to create businesses, graduate from college, serve on boards, and live useful lives. "It had a happy ending", Hart says of the four years that the school operated outside the district. Its success opened the arms of the community to the power of education. Faith was refired.

As an undergraduate at University of Wisconsin-Whitewater, I was able to participate in a program that certified its graduates for teaching underprivileged children. The experience changed my life. Reading Leo Hart's story reminds me of the principles that were taught to all of us rural college interns who knew their cows, but didn't know about gangs. Like Hart, we wanted to see the potential in every child being realized. It became our passion in life.

> *Woody Guthrie was an Okie. He sang the songs that the migrant workers from the Dust Bowl recognized. Guthrie's experience as an emigrant to California mirrored those of the Weedpatch Camp: loss of dignity, deprivation and hopelessness. In his songs, Guthrie expressed these emotions. "They say I'm a dust bowl refugee, and I ainta gonna be treated this way." Those words from the song,* **"Goin' Down This Old Dusty Road"** *spoke to the Okies who had lost everything in the Dust Bowl and gained hardships in California.*

In the novel, **Dust Between the Stitches**, the residents of Hooverville long to travel to California to get a job and have a better life.

Jerry Stanley's book, **Children of the Dust Bowl**, describes the work of Leo Hart from interviews and research that Stanley conducted.

Chapter Ten
5 Lessons for Today's Teachers from Weedpatch Camp School

5 LESSONS FOR TODAY'S TEACHERS

From Weedpatch Camp School

During the darkest days of the Great Depression, thousands of Oklahoma families migrated from the Dust Bowl to California in automobiles piled high with their earthly belongings. The grove owners and truck farmers referred to the penniless refugees from drought as "Okies". The name carried prejudice toward the migrants trying to escape starvation by working for pennies in the California fields.

The children of these tent dwellers needed an education. Leo Hart gathered fifty ragtag youngsters with a group of dedicated teachers and built Weedpatch Camp School. From the heart wrenching triumph of this educational experiment, the current crop of teachers in the United States could learn five valuable lessons in how to change lives with the right mix of chalk and challenge.

The first lesson to be gleaned from Leo Hart and his staff is a philosophical one. It underlies every curriculum decision, every daily lesson plan, as well as the manner in which the students are embraced. Leo Hart believed that every child is capable of learning and therefore deserved a good education. Leo Hart gazed beyond the ill-fitting feed sack dresses, holey overalls, unwashed bodies, slimy hair and green teeth. He saw raw potential that needed to be unleashed. Youngsters with the same dreams and hopes as kids everywhere. Too often, teachers judge children by social class, zip code, or religious affiliation. They fail to visualize the transformation of a mind in the hands of a caring educator.

In the words of Haim Garrett: "Treat a child as though he already is the person he's capable of becoming."

The second lesson involved changing the curriculum to meet the needs of the child. Teachers often quote, "If a child can't learn the way we teach them, then change the way you teach." Leo Hart and his faculty developed daily plans designed to civilize the migrant camp kid. Janitors taught school cobbling so the students could repair their shoes. Girls learned to sew and fit the feed sack material used for their clothing. The recipe for toothpaste and its use was demonstrated Self-sufficiency was taught as the fifty youngsters raised livestock, planted gardens, and cooked meals. The staff and pupils built the school from bricks, orange crates, and surplus lumber which developed carpentry skills. Because most students barely knew the alphabet or basic arithmetic, Hart developed lesson plans on their levels. The teachers taught math, reading, writing, history, art and music that challenged the untapped waif's minds.

Arriving at Weedpatch Camp from Oklahoma Photo by Dorothea Lange

Robert John Meechem expressed the concept in these words. "Each day we must put forth a greater effort than we're capable of doing. We can never limit ourselves to do what teachers have done in the past."

The most common-sense lesson that Leo Hart taught his staff was that underfed children find learning difficult. To boost the general health of the children, orange juice and cod liver oil were given in abundance. The school offered a hot breakfast for a penny, and a hot lunch for two cents. Because malnourishment is fatiguing, one hour of rest helped the children stay alert. Eventually, most of the food eaten at the school was grown in the garden, found in the chicken coops or milked from goats and cows. Lessons in health and organic eating.

Jim Hunt believes that "teachers have the hardest and most important jobs in America. They're building our nation."

Photo by Dorothea Lange

The fourth lesson Leo Hart believed as essential to educating student involved their parents. Every weekend, Leo worked with the parents to build the school. Many of the fathers possessed skills essential to laying water pipes and stringing electrical wires. Edna Hart, Leo's wife, stayed in the kitchen with the women and canned beets and cooked meals while listening to their country dialects. Because the parents became invested in the school, they stayed longer, trying to find work locally so their offspring could continue in school.

"Every child in your class is someone's whole world."- Anonymous

Jane D. Hull obviously worked with parents. "At the end of the day, the most overwhelming key to a child's success is the positive involvement of parents."

The final lesson exemplified at Weedpatch Camp School was one of ownership. The students loved their school, their staff, and their opportunity to learn. No more fists raised in anger. No more bullying. The students dug ditches for water lines, scooped out latrines, and created a swimming pool. When their Friday grades reached a high level, they drove the C-46 airplane (where they had classes) up and down the runway. Leo bragged that "we left everything lying around and no one ever stole a thing." Respect for the school was hard earned, but proved to be valuable.

Carlton Faulconer graduated from Weedpatch Camp School and from Bakersfield Junior College. He realized the gift given to him as an Oakie. "The school gave us pride and dignity and honor when we didn't have these things. We were special."

The five lessons from Weedpatch Camp School flow from a long line of teachers who were born to teach. People like Leo Hart. People like Fredrick Douglass, who realized that "it is easier to build strong children, than to repair broken men and women." It was true then. It is truer now.

Chapter Eleven
Radio: The Voices from the Air

"You gain strength, courage and confidence by every experience in which you really stoop to look fear in the face. You must do the thing which you think you cannot do."

-Eleanor Roosevelt, wife of President Franklin D. Roosevelt

Life in the dust bowl on isolated homesteads presented challenges to the lonely farmers and their wives. At the beginning of the 1930's, twelve million households owned a radio. By 1939, over twenty-eight million families gathered around the central piece of the living room to take their minds off the plunging prices of crops, the relentless drought, and to release their fears from the Black Blizzards. The "talking telegram" provided mental health to those who tottered on the cusp of despair.

"Laughter is a good medicine." That's why the dials stayed on the stations where a belly laugh was guaranteed. Comedians such as Jack Benny, Fibber McGee, and Fred Allen brought smiles to sun dried, tight lips. Somehow, the difficulties faced in the light of cloudless days mellowed in the mirth of evening shadows. A healthy dose of laughter each day boosted spirits.

Drama set the imagination free, taking the listener to a place where problems were solved. The Lone Ranger and The Shadow sparked a sense of adventure. "Our Gal Sunday" and "One Man's Family" provided soap opera appeal which brought listeners back every week to continue the story filled with melodrama.

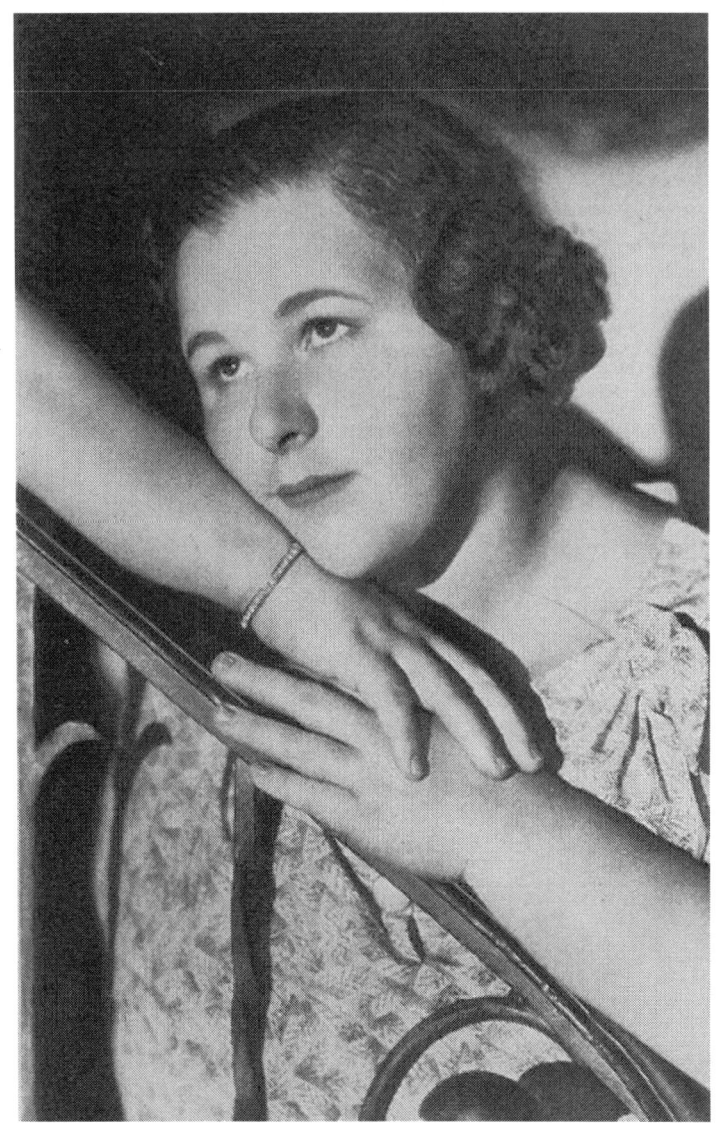

Kate Smith – National Archives

Music captivated the soul of the audiences who sang along with the radio voices. Roy Rogers and Dale Evans encouraged dust-weary folks with their homespun charm. Dale Evans advised, "The cowgirl faces life head on, lives by her own lights and makes no excuses." Roy would tell the cow punchers in radio land that it was "all in the way that you ride the trail that counts." As they sang "Happy Trails to You" in two-part harmony, Roy and Dale inspired homesteaders face the future with courage.

The Carter Family belted out one gospel tune after another, bringing spiritual uplift to the beaten down listeners. "Will the Circle Be Unbroken?" became a signature Carter song, reminding westerners of the fragility of life and the serious business of the soul. June Carter once said, "Life has a habit of not staying hitched. You got to ride it like you find it."

Woody Guthrie sang his gritty songs on radio, appealing to the Oakies and their constant battle with poverty. A calming voice, Kate Smith dug deep into her passion for life and inspired listeners with her version of "God Bless America." Other groups brought mixtures of love and "crying in the beer" songs that moved the people across the west to join in with gusto and tears.

Perhaps the most important use of the radio encapsulated keeping in touch with the President. During the Great Depression, Franklin Roosevelt initiated his "fireside chats", which helped an entire hurting nation to feel the heartbeat of their leader. For a struggling nation, a memorable fireside chat was transmitted on September 6, 1936 when the President described the Dust Bowl conditions he observed firsthand on a tour of the devastated area. He addressed the fears and concerns of an increasingly distraught populace with a steady voice and calming words. The depth of the anxiety of the drought ridden homesteader grew easier after the President spoke these words: "There is nothing to fear but fear itself."

Radio played an important role in bringing together a nation on the brink of disaster. As technology has advanced, the "golden age of radio" will be remembered as the bandage for a hurting nation. Tonight, as the music and commentators amuse me while I prepare supper, I will enter into the magic of radio. A companion that talks about hog prices and local crime. The sounds of music that keep my dishwashing routine going. A reminder that in my daily life filled with drama and trauma, I need to be connected.

"I never forget that I live in a house owned by all the American people and that I have been given their trust."-President Franklin D. Roosevelt

Chapter Twelve
Piecing a Legacy: A 1930 Quilt Story

Piecing a Legacy: A 1930's Dust Bowl Quilt

With the perspective of youth, Dennis McCann observed, "Those must have been depressing times, those long-ago days of bread and milk, of feedbag clothes, and canned tumbleweed dinners. Of little or nothing." Jane Tamse countered in her feeble, quivering voice, "Those were frugal days, but they left us with a happy childhood."

Making of Memories

I ran across this piece of advice in a sewing book. *"Stitch *together scraps of family love into a warm memory quilt that cradles in its folds encouragement and truth that still apply."*

When my mother passed away, I was thirty-three years old. One of the bags in her back closet held muslin feed sacks cut into 12-inch squares with a stack of 48 state bird/flower transfers to be ironed onto the material for embroidering. With three small children, I started the project, then laid down the needle for thirty years.

My granddaughter, Kaeley, started attending the local quilting club, Stitchers, with me after I retired from teaching. I finished embroidering 24 of the squares, making a State Bird/Flower Sampler. Under the guidance of master quilters, Kaeley sewed the feed sack material into a thing of beauty. As a college student, Kaeley sleeps under a quilt started by her great-grandmother of the 1930's, embroidered by her grandmother, and stitched by herself. A lot of love wrapped up in that comforter.

Piecing Together a Life

Quilts remind me that all the scraps and pieces of shredded longings and tattered lives can somehow be stitched together into a beautiful display. The people of the Dust Bowl experienced brokenness. The dreams of their youth were unfulfilled by the circumstances that hammered them and tore their aspirations into shreds. Farmers lost their livelihoods which shattered their dignity. For the first time in American history, middle class workers lived one paycheck from destitution. Homemakers gathered scraps of materials to create the necessities of life. Relationships grew ragged under the strain of constant deprivation. Hope frayed into thread strips of despair.

But God, the ultimate source of Creativity, views this brokenness as pre-art. God uses the patterns of *repentance-forgiveness* and *trust-obey* as He hovers over scrappy lives with a heart of compassion itching to make art out of every tear, every shredded dream, every unfulfilled dream. From these ragged scraps, He creates a design of usefulness and beauty from our messy lives. Those children who grew up in deprivation were pieced together into patterns that shaped them into adults who took on responsibility without flinching.

The Greatest Generation

From the challenging childhoods of the Great Depression and Dust Bowl emerged a group of people who met life headlong without fear. We call them the Greatest Generation.

The finished quilt started by Cleo's mother in the Dust Bowl with feed sack muslin squares and transfers from newspapers.

Chapter Thirteen
A Picture Worth Thousands of Words: The Dust Bowl by Ken Burns

For two hours, Vernon and I watched disturbing, yet stunning visuals flash across our television screen. Frightening images of gigantic black blizzards engulfing barns and cities with devastating results. Plagues of jackrabbits and locusts. Old and young coughing from dust pneumonia. The first DVD of **The Dust Bowl**, by Ken Burns, sent chills pearling over our spines and minds. Through personal interviews with survivors of the 1930's, private letters, newspaper accounts and compelling photos,

Ken Burns sets out the causes of the worst catastrophe in ecological history in the United States. With iconic photos and news films from the day, the documentary huddled Vernon and I together on our couch as the life stories of unimaginable human suffering filled us with grief and shock.

The Songs of the Damned

Probably the most disconcerting aspect of Part I of **The Dust Bowl** was the music. The persons in the interviews recall hymns being sung by their parents during the worst of the droughts. Woody Guthrie sang "So Long, It's Been Good to Know You" a song he wrote as he sat at a kitchen table believing the end of the world was at hand. In the background of the film, a dulcimer played "Bringing in The Sheaves" as the visuals presented more mile-high dust storms, dead livestock and leathered homesteaders. The disconnect between the song and the reality of the situation heightened our depression as Vernon and I watched thousands of desperate families who faced poverty, foreclosure, starvation and death. Most of all, they tackled fear of the unknown. Every day. On frayed threads of hope.

The End of the Story

It took courage to watch Part 2 of **The Dust Bowl**. But the possibility that there was a solution to an unsolvable situation intrigued both Vernon and me. While watching the efforts of President Franklin D. Roosevelt to marshal government efforts to help the farmers who lost 850 million tons of topsoil in one year, I learned to appreciate this man known for his calming Fireside Chats.

THE DUST BOWL: LIVING IN TOUGH TIMES

National Archives

But the stories of Henry Finnell and Hugh Bennett are what caught my attention, because these men lifted my heart. They embodied the concept of preparation for "such a time as this" by a providential God. Both Finnell and Bennett possessed the exact scientific backgrounds needed to turn around the results of man's greed. The story of the dust bowl, which had been so scary and humbling, finally morphed into a realization of the hand of God in the affairs of man. A sense of hope.

Lessons Learned

The dust bowl is an overlooked era in American history. By watching this documentary, my husband and I learned so much about man's relationship to the land, and the limits of government. We recognized the human capacity for perseverance despite incredible suffering. We acknowledged the providence of God in the affairs of man. The unforgettable images, stories and music of that era fill my heart with admiration for the people of that time and provide insights into the uncertain future our nation faces today.

A sobering film of Ken Burns' finest work.

Chapter Fourteen
Bon Appetite: Depression Style

Should I steal when I'm hungry?

The boys in my class for behavior disordered students always had the same question. Each year.

"What do you do when you don't have nothing to eat at home?"

Usually, this led to a discussion on why it is all right to steal from the local 7-Eleven because the store has a lot of food and makes enough money to share. Urban situation ethics. I tried to steer their thinking into creative cooking, a skill I learned from my mother. No five-finger discount.

Basic ingredients

There were times when my mother created edible food out of very basic ingredients. As a young bride in 1930's Dust Bowl, she learned to serve meals with no refrigeration, far from a grocery store, with a tiny sheepherder's stove. Sort of like camping every day, trying to give a man who will work for 12 hours on a dragline. Like other homemakers in the Great Depression, mealtime became a constant challenge of supply and demand, little money, sparse gardens.

The pantry staple started with buckwheat flour for pancakes, flipped for breakfast, lunch or dinner. A supply of cornmeal mush doused in syrup filled empty breakfast tummies, then left over mush fried for supper finished the day. Another kitchen "must-have" included oatmeal. Anita Nevin's mother put plumped up raisins in the oatmeal on Sunday as a treat. With these three items on the shelf, everyone ate.

With a bit of flour, an egg and salt, homemade noodles were rolled out, cut in strips and dried on towel covered chairs for several hours. Versatile, these hearty noodles were used in soups, main dishes with bacon grease, garnished with dried bread crumbs, backed with apple sliced in. Noodles in yummy hot dishes stretched bits of veggies, ham or chicken into a belly filling hot casserole.

Linen lifters for nutrition

No meal planning was complete without a good recipe for baked beans. The ingredients varied, but most were tasty and nourishing. Beans replaced meat, an expensive food item. As I read letters to my mother, written in the 1930's, my grandmother and grandfather each had a pork chop to celebrate their wedding anniversary. In the Dust Bowl area, the standard meal was "Jack, biscuits and beans." The "Jack" was, of course, jackrabbit.

Dandelions, lamb's quarters and tumble weed leaves all supplied "greens" for salads. An acquired taste.

Meals remembered

Here are quotes from adults who remember home cooked means in the 1930's.

"Rabbits and squirrels fried and made gravy."-Doris Conte

"Every family knew what it was to live on bread and gravy."-Delores Harris

"As a girl, I remember carrying a glass jar of cooked oatmeal and the teacher put it in a dish pan of hot water."-Verna Lindsay

"Lunch for school was homemade bread with lard and syrup."-Enid Dresmel

"We ate a lot of bread pudding because we had bread, eggs and milk." –Audrey Samplowski

The students in my class reluctantly admitted that if there were no food in their house, they went to their grandmother or auntie's homes. If nothing else, they made a batch of macaroni and tomatoes or fried eggs and toast.

Now that sounds like Depression food.

Chapter Fifteen
Feeding the Mind: Pack Horse Library Project

"With no money to feed the body, how could they feed the mind?"- Eleanor Roosevelt

Wanted: Librarians

The search for dedicated women to serve as librarians began with the impetus of Eleanor Roosevelt as she cooperated with the WPA, Work Project Administration. The WPA was created by her husband, President Franklin Delano Roosevelt, as a way to get men back to work in

1935 when the country tottered on the brink of starvation. But Eleanor knew that women could not do the backbreaking hard labor in the WPA, so she encouraged the creation of jobs for the many women now heading households. Meaningful tasks that utilized their skills: health services, school lunch programs, sewing projects, and libraries.

Riding into Isolated Hollows

That's when the Pack Horse Library Project of Eastern Kentucky was conceived. Eleanor realized the difficult road ahead for the librarians on horseback because there were no paved or gravel roads in that section of Kentucky. Or telephones, or newspapers, or radios. A section of terrain with one-room school houses hugging the incline. Mining camps dotting the flat areas. Weathered wooden cabins nestling near crooks and hollows that cut the populace from the outside world. Mountain folk hungry not only for vittles, but for nourishment of their imaginations and knowledge.

Pack horse librarians were a gritty breed. For $28 a month, they traveled on rocky terrain in all kinds of weather with saddlebags filled with books and magazines. The creek beds named Hell-For-Sartin, Troublesome and Cut Shin hampered their weekly treks of 50-80 miles, but the librarians persevered because they were committed to the value of their job. They were feeding the minds of Kentucky's mountain folk with the power of words to transcend daily life.

The Hunger of Mind and Soul

The librarians discovered that magazines were most appreciated because they provided information needed for those hungering to improve their life skills. Short articles on health care, cooking, agriculture or machinery added to the isolated folk's knowledge. Those individuals starved for pictures to help with the reading process enjoyed the children's books. The youngsters who longed to fill their minds with imagination read aloud to their younger siblings, as well as the older people whose educations had been inadequate. Literacy entered the valleys as the saddle laden horses made their appointed rounds. What these librarians accomplished could not be measured in money because they gave no less than the keys to the world.

There were two problems that the mountain folk complained about to the pack horse librarians. First, the cost of additional lamp oil needed to read in the long winter nights. Second, the difficulty of getting the children out of bed in the morning after they read "just one more chapter.

The program lost its funding in 1943 due to the war. It is estimated that 100,000 folks participated in the library services during the eight years that the pack horse librarians brought the power of the written page to miners, parents, preschoolers and children of the Kentucky hills. As Gladys Lainhart, a pack horse worker commented: "It would be difficult to estimate how much this good work is doing to brighten the lives of the people in our Kentucky mountains."

How does anyone measure a mind set free to dream and wonder?

As an elementary student, our family lived in rural areas with one-room schoolhouses with limited libraries. The bookmobile brought two crates of books biweekly. I read most of them from cover to cover, crying when Meg died in **Little Women**, *becoming compassionate toward animals through* **Black Beauty**, *laughing at Henry Huggins, and dreaming of adventures with Thor Heyderdahl and the* **Seven Wonders of the Ancient World**. *The bookmobile allowed this ex-teacher a chance to dream. -Cleo Lampos*

Down Cut Shin Creek by Kathi Appelt and Jeanne Cannella Schmitzer tells the true stories of the pack horse librarians.

Wonderland Creek, by Lynn Austin, is historical fiction at its best as a young girl from Blue Island, Illinois, is recruited to be a pack horse librarian in Kentucky.

Chapter Sixteen
Dust Bowl: Photojournalists

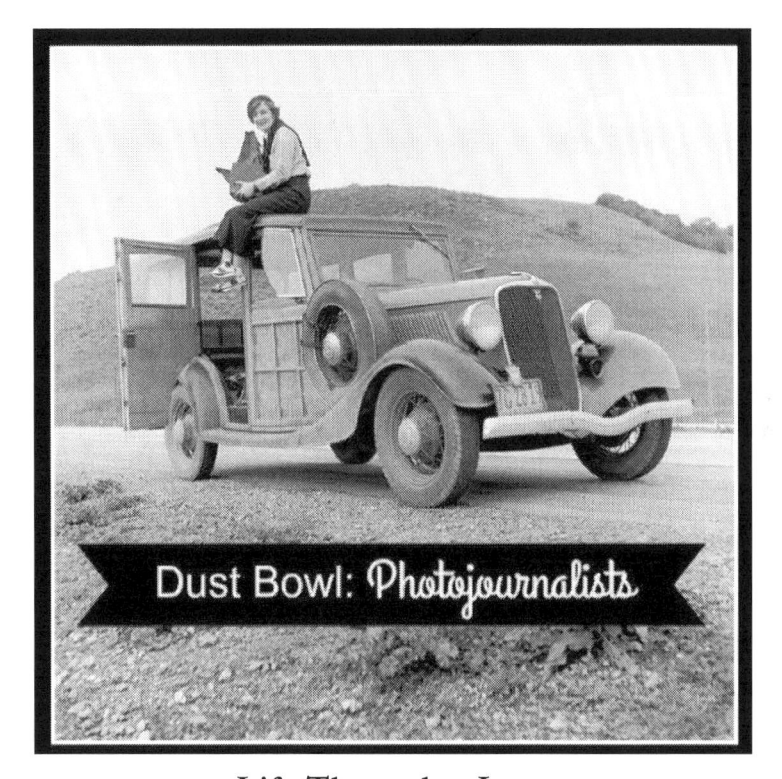

Life Through a Lens

"Speak up for those who cannot speak for themselves - for the rights of all who are destitute." Proverbs 31:8

Ever wonder who took the iconic photos from the Dust Bowl that make our hearts ache and give us nightmares? A few pioneers in a new field of photo documentary brought this era to life for the people of the 1930's, and provided haunting images for this generation to ponder.

The FSA, Farm Security Administration, conscripted a team of young photographers to take their cameras and talent to the impoverished farmers and ranchers and record their daily struggles. They wanted to visualize the problems facing those in the Dust Bowl, and then record how the government was intervening. These young unemployed shutter snappers leaped at the opportunity to hone their craft, make a living, and travel to the middle of the country. What they viewed from the lenses of their equipment sobered their minds and troubled their hearts. Their experiences in the Dust Bowl changed their lives.

A Heart for People

Dorothea Lange, as a twenty-year-old, took compelling photos of the pain and misery of men and women who had lost everything. Their haunting eyes are captured in her iconic black and white compositions, stirring the empathy of the public in urban areas who suffered from the Great Depression. Her photos defined the desperation of the Dust Bowl.

A twenty-two-year-old from the Bronx, Arthur Rothstein had to learn how to drive a car in order to be hired by the FSA. Arthur was assigned to the heart of the Dust Bowl, along with Henry Finnell, the soil conservationist who worked with the farmers and ranchers to reclaim their soil.

A farmer and his two sons during a dust storm in Cimarron County, Oklahoma, 1936, Photo: Arthur Rothstein

The starkness of his landscapes depicted the depth of the difficulties faced by the people of the land. Several of his pictures portrayed the misery and terrors of the Dust Bowl in ways that Finnell's words could not. Despite the devastation and despair that became Arthur's daily portion as he walked with Finnell and the destitute farmers, he remained optimistic. "I have found that if you love life, life will love you back."

A Lifetime Dedicated to Capturing History

This team of young people invented new processes in photography. All of them continued in the work of documenting society as they recorded the Japanese internment camps, the Liberators of Nazi death camps, the race riots of the 50's and 60's, and the Frozen Chosen in the Korean Conflict. The importance of these photojournalists' contributions is demonstrated by the emotional response that their work conveys as it is still shown all over the world.

"Broke, baby sick, and car trouble!" - Dorothea Lange's 1937 photo of a Missouri migrant family's jalopy stuck near Tracy, California.

"I am trying here to say something about the despised, the defeated, the alienated. About death and disaster, about the wounded, the crippled, the rootless, the dislocated. About finality. About the last ditch."- Dorothea Lange

Chapter Seventeen
Dust Bowl: From CCC to Greatest Generation

The family's farm is in foreclosure. Dust storms blot out the sun and bury the livestock. The older siblings try to share their beans, biscuit and Jack with the younger ones who cry themselves to sleep on empty stomachs. Dad's eyes stare blankly at the dried-out landscape. Mom is quiet, her graying hair pulled into a bun. Going to school barefoot with no supplies doesn't make sense. What's a teenage boy to do?

Many young men turned to the opportunity for self-respect that the CCC, Civilian Conservation Corps, offered in these difficult times. Under the sponsorship of President Roosevelt, the CCC lasted from 1933 to 1942 as a public work relief program. It reached out to unemployed, unmarried men whose families were on relief. For the 17-28 year olds, the CCC represented hope. Malnourished, poorly clothed and under-educated, the young men arrived at the barrack type compounds that ran with military precision. After eating three meals a day, dressing out in new uniforms, and sleeping on a bunk, these young men gained work experience, additional education, and lots of self-confidence. Of the $30 they earned each month, $25 was sent to their families. For these recruits, helping out the folks was a privilege.

Imagine the over three million men who participated in the CCC and accomplished a legacy of production that still stands today. They worked with Henry Finnell in the Dust Bowl, learning about soil conservation and helping to teach the farmers. They built muscles by planting a windbreak on the Great Plains that stretched from Texas to Canada. They learned to operate bulldozers to level sand dunes. Their efforts were integral to Henry Finnell's ability to implement radical conservation changes that turned around the devastation of the Dust Bowl. All across America, the CCC worked in conservation and infrastructure projects that are still used today.

The CCC ended in 1942 when the WWII started. The disciplined training and physical fitness of these workers coincided seamlessly with recruitment into the armed forces. These men who were former children of the Dust Bowl had grown up with tough exteriors that protected their inner dreams and sensitive emotions from being extinguished as they faced one disappointment after another growing up. Their childhoods were forged on the anvil of hardship by the hammer of frugality. Rising from the grit of their teen years, the CCC prepared millions of these men to take on the challenges of Nazi Germany. They stormed the beaches of Normandy, raised the flag on Iwo Jima, liberated death camps, and returned to the States.

Ready to live their lives, these men married, raised large families, built schools, led Little League teams, served on church boards, and ran for political offices. The difficulties of their childhood predisposed them for the unique legacy as a generation who were duty bound to serve others and pass on a priceless heritage of strong values. These kids of the Dust Bowl who served in the CCC became what will be forever known as The Greatest Generation.

From the Dust Bowl to CCC to WWII to Greatest Generation. Salute.

"This enterprise (CCC) is an established part of our national policy. It will conserve our precious natural resources. It will pay dividends to the present and future generations. It will make improvements in national and state domains which have been largely forgotten in the past few years of industrial development.

More important, however, than the material gains will be the moral and spiritual value of such work. The overwhelming majority of unemployed Americans, who are now walking the streets and receiving private or public relief, would infinitely preferred to work. We can take a vast army of these unemployed out into healthful surroundings. We can eliminate to some extent at least the threat that enforced idleness brings to spiritual and moral stability. It is not a panacea for all the unemployment but it is an essential step in this emergency." - President Franklin Delano Roosevelt

President Franklin Roosevelt visited with CCC enrollees near Camp Roosevelt on August 12, 1933, at Big Meadows, Skyland Drive, Virginia. Seated from left are Maj. Gen. Paul B. Malone, Louis M. Howe, Harold L. Ickes, Robert Fechner, FDR, Henry A. Wallace, and Rexford Tugwell. (35-GE-3A-5) National Archives

Chapter Eighteen
Coloring Christmas Orange:
Celebrating in the Great Depression

Coloring Christmas Orange: Celebrating in the Great Depression

The one thing that every family in the 1930's Dust Bowl savored for Christmas was an orange. In our own culture of entitlement and excess, the thought of one orange constituting the holiday pay load is unimaginable. But getting an orange was a big deal because citrus fruit wasn't affordable during the rest of the year. Tom Heck, a Wisconsin dairy farmer, shares how his mother was so grateful to get one because she "knew that her parents had sacrificed to buy the oranges." Like all children, she hoped that a banana, nuts and candy would be stuffed into the stocking, also.

The Great Depression lasted ten years with over 25% of the work force without jobs. The middle class became poor, but the poor drowned into desperation. Soup kitchens and bread lines sprung up in every city. With necessities barely in reach, gift giving required imagination. Flour sacks were saved to stitch a dress for girls or an apron for a woman. Boys and men received knitted scarves and mittens. Underwear or socks purchases provided a practical present. Homemade soap was popular.

Wrapping gifts pushed frugality. Year after year, the same wrapping paper enclosed presents, forcing the recipient to carefully lift tape, remove the paper and fold it for next year. If the paper showed wrinkles, a gentle iron flattened it out. The colorful Sunday comics supplied a stack of wrapping that could be ripped off. The white paper from the butcher allowed a background for potato stamping or attaching cut outs with flour paste. Attractive packages emerged from creative hands.

For those who brought small trees or tumbleweeds into the home to decorate, paper chains from catalog pages, wooden carved ornaments, or pine cones made the Christmas trees festive. The tree created a focal point for the card playing, singing, and eating of the traditional chicken dinner with the relatives who gathered for fellowship after church services. The real significance of the holiday rested in the hope represented by the coming of the Babe in the manger. As the children of the Dust Bowl grew up, what they remembered best were their extended families, fun, and togetherness; not the gifts, trees and tinsel. They didn't have much as children. But, maybe, they had much more.

Photo by Carl Mydans

"They were very rough times," said Clarence Jamison Sr. who would be toughened by the Great Depression to become one of the famed Tuskegee Airman of WWII. "We usually got something practical like long underwear or a pair of shoes for the year."

Eugen Lyons recalls his single mother raising three children. "There wasn't much levity in that household, but there was always hope." And no Christmas tree. "We'd have burned that for heat in the potbellied stove."

Mother and Baby of Family of Nine, Carl Mydans, Library of Congress

As a high school student in Texas, Beverly Roberts Jostad worked with her home economic classes to make new dresses for some pre-loved dolls. The shop classes turned out toy trucks and games for children. Then the students distributed the gifts to needy families. Beverly wasn't prepared for the last delivery of small packages and a box of groceries. Barely a shack, the students approached the dwelling with smoke rising from the stack. A young woman opened the door with a girl of 2, and boys perhaps 4 and 5 years old peeking around her skirt. They entered at the woman's invitation.

Beverly tells the story. "I knelt to reach the little girl. The linoleum floor was worn but spotless. Bleached flour-sack curtains hung at the windows. Neatly made beds occupied one corner of the room and the kitchen another. A small stove furnished heat.

As I turned to the children, dressed in clean, neatly patched clothes, I noticed several green tree branches standing upright in a dirt-filled pot. A red cloth circled the base. Can lids and paper angels hung on string and a tiny paper star graced the treetop. Streamers of popcorn completed the decorations.

The room was silent as the children looked at their mother, wondering if the gifts were really for them. The little girl hugged the doll and the boy grasped the trucks as they sought an answer. The mother put her arms around them and said in a choked voice, 'I told you Santa Claus would come.'" Beverly still tears at the memory of that family.

Annie Hiller sums up the feelings of most Greatest Generation men and women. "Mama presented us with what I now know were very special gifts: the gift of music as she played her little accordion and we sang, the gift of stories about the First Christmas, and the gift of enjoyment in playing games together. No family was ever more abundantly blessed, for in our poverty, we had Mama."

An orange in a stocking. It was enough. It was everything.

Chapter Nineteen
Stitches in Time

In most cultures, the older women pass on the skills they have acquired over a lifetime to the next generation like a needle pulling thread in a running stitch. Just as my life as a mother and wife started and my mother's wealth of knowledge of all things domestic was needed, she passed over Jordan and left me with a bag of washed, ironed and neatly folded chicken feed bags. Vintage ones. Depression/Dust Bowl era muslin. In addition to the organic fabric, the bag held forty-eight ink transfers collected one by one from a newspaper. Each decal depicted the official bird and flower of the pre-Alaska/Hawaii States of America. Raised with the Puritan work ethic of busy hands, my mother hand-stitched even stamp sized fabric into useable comforters. Obviously, she intended on making a quilt by embroidering the squares then sewing them together. I wanted to weep over her lifetime of unfulfilled dreams as my three-year-old son asked, "What's in the bag, Mommy?"

Getting Started

It took a few months to go to the fabric store and purchase the hoop, needles, embroidery floss and little scissors needed to start the project. At age 33, the recollections of the fine points of stitchery learned while living with my Aunt Lois needed dusting. Aunt Lois lived to hand stitch. In the evenings, Aunt Lois told me what color thread to put in the needles that her nimble fingers pressed along blue inked designs in pillow case and tea towel material. She taught me to make French Knots and keep my stitches tiny and on the blue stenciled line. I learned from a master embroiderer.

Now, the work required me to go it alone. Beset by the pressures of busyness, I decided to double the thread, causing my stitches to rise above the cloth like nubby scars from deep wounds on toughened skin. An interesting outline of the birds and flowers emerged in bias relief. One that any Braille student's fingers could read accurately. Ten squares resulted from the three years of sewing before I worked on my Master's Degree and my children oozed into their teen years. Then the bag of fabric and thread was stuffed and forgotten in the back of the closet while a crazy quilt of activities overtook my life.

The Tyranny of Time

Fast forward thirty frantic, fearful and fun years raising a family, teaching special needs children and becoming Glam-ma. No time for embroidering birds or state flowers. My husband and I joined a church down the street from us, and one of the gathering places for women was the Stitchers Club. Crochet, embroidery, tatting, knitting, cross stitch and quilting. Joyce Beenes invited me to come, and so the search for the bag of feed sack cloth began. After cleaning out a few closets, the remnants of a project emerged. The women didn't laugh, but most had no idea that chicken feed sacks existed, much less served as fodder for sewing. Raised in the city, they traveled to quilt stores all over the Midwest to procure their fabrics. As I sat at the table talking to the Stitchers, they accepted the oddity of my project. Joyce and her friend, Jan Bos, encouraged me to persevere as they finished quilt after quilt.

For four years, every second Friday of the month, I trudged to the fellowship hall and sat among the sewing machines and hand sewers. The rhythmic hum of the machines created a conversational backdrop for the older members of the group. Marge Speelman especially drew me to her side as she told story after story of living in "the old neighborhood" of Englewood/Roseland and raising her children. The difficulty of providing for private Christian school educations for all of them. The faithfulness of God to meet her needs. As her crochet needles clicked slower and the stories were repeated in a predictable loop, Marge stitched her heart to mine and presented me with a love for God deeper than words could express. Her passing left and empty chair and an empty place in my soul. I realized how much the older women from the Greatest Generation taught me about how to live as our needles wove hues of color on blank cloth.

Renewed Spirit

During this time, my husband and I trekked across the Rocky Mountains to visit my brother-in-law in Nevada. At the Colorado Welcome Center, on a huge wall, the finished version of my quilt hung. All fifty states, carefully threaded by volunteers who joined them in a colorful display. Stepping close, I noted the workmanship. No bias relief outline stitches. Every bird and flower was perfectly detailed with filled in hues of finely sewn threads. I knew what I had to do.

Embroidering the squares began in earnest. Taking out the encyclopedia, I copied the colors of the bird's feathers with my thread, shading in light and dark tones. The flowers, too, burst alive with subtle color changes. The contrast of the outlined figures completed in my youth with the filled in ones recently done, created a kind of schizophrenic combination, as if two completely different individuals had threaded the squares. But that part appeared somewhat true, as my personality over the thirty odd years had changed drastically from an anxious young mother to a settled Glam-ma.

A New Generation of Stitchers

By now, 26 squares lay finished in my basket. A far cry from the 48 possibilities. But help arrived in the form of my 15-year-old granddaughter, Kaeley, who wanted to learn to sew. I figured that the straight stitching of joining posts and sashes would be a foundational start. Little did I know. On the first session, Kaeley took my completed state bird and flower squares and mapped them out on the rug. For an hour, she arranged and rearranged them until a visually balanced rectangle lay on the floor. Snatching her cell phone, she snapped a picture for later reference in laying out the quilt. To the delight of Joyce and Jan, Kaeley became invested in her great-grandmother's dust bowl project that night.

A year of sewing followed. Some months Kaeley's teen life did not allow a trip to Stitchers, but most months, she showed up and ran the sewing machine through its paces. A perfectionist, she took out wonky threads. Jan and Joyce guided her through every new process. Every nuance of quilting. Every trick of the trade.

Cleo Lampos with her granddaughter and the finished quilt started by Cleo's mother in the Dust Bowl with feed sack muslin squares and transfers from newspapers.

Soon the dog feed was changed and Kaeley meandered over fabric, creating flowerlettes as she sewed. I heard a knitter comment, "That girl is fearless." She was. And she was filled with pride as the last stitch locked into the sash. At age sixteen, Kaeley rose above her peers as the only one who owned a sewing machine and had pieced together a quilt. Kaeley, an art major in college, sleeps under the cottony love of her great-grandmother and her Glam-ma. She finished a dream that started three generations before her. She sleeps under a quilt that Joyce and Jan guided into completion. These two women shared the knowledge of their years of sewing with a novice. A teenager. They did this out of a passion for quilting and for the joy of watching the next generation take up the thread and needle in a creative manner. The older women teaching the younger women to dream in fabrics, designs and colors.

Stitches in time.

Chapter Twenty
Irish Immigration and the Orphan Trains Changed the Direction of my Life

The gift shop shelves heaved with books covered by grainy photos of children huddled around coal driven steam engines. Dressed in turn of the century clothes, some ragamuffins carried grief like luggage, but others appeared wide-eyed with adventure. "Orphan trains," my brother explained. "Those children were adopted here in the St. Cloud, Minnesota area. They spoke in the school system for years about their experiences." I bought an armload of books.

Endless Homeless Children

Subsequent research detailed how an average of 300 homeless urchins every month for 70 years rode the orphan trains. Did anyone miss even one of these children? They escaped from Five Points, New York City to be adopted by church sponsored families on farms in the Midwest. The flow stopped in 1930. But what kind of mother put children on these trains, and how well did the children do in their new homes?

The Birth of Foster Care

For two years, I read every book, magazine article, or Google account. My husband and I attended the Little Falls Orphan Train Reunion and met four elderly riders. We traveled to Concordia, Kansas, and researched at the Orphan Train Museum. Then, I realized how the suffering of Irish immigrant women contributed to the homeless waifs overflowing onto the streets of New York City. Women who could no longer care for their children gave them up to the chance of a new life through what we now call foster or adoptive agencies.

Reading the accounts of these riders as they tried to assimilate into the Midwest proved to be inspiring and heart wrenching. Most eventually made the transition. Some never did. The adoptive families faced overwhelming challenges. But, agents of the Children's Aid Society, like Clara Comstock, rode the train with the children, settled them into their homes, and checked on them every year.

These agents introduced the class of social workers of today with their grit and determination to meet the needs of traumatized children.

Spreading the Story

Of course, a book, **A Mother's Song**, resulted from this research. The overflow of knowledge produced published magazine articles and chances to speak to senior classes, book clubs, and genealogy groups. I have met so many interesting people because of these opportunities to write and speak as a retired educator.

An awareness of how Irish immigration led to the greatest movement of children in the United States has been the result of my search into history. And it all started in the gift shop of a museum.

"The work was a great adventure in Faith: we were always helped and grew to expect kindness, deep interest and assistance everywhere. We were constantly attempting the impossible…I thought it the most incredible thing imaginable to expect people to take children they had never seen and give them a home, but we placed them and never failed to accomplish it."- *Clara Comstock's speech in 1931 to Children's Aid Society Staff*

Chapter Twenty-One
Singing in Hard Times

The conditions of the Dust Bowl pressed the farmers and ranchers into despair. Too many days with the sun blocked out by the Black Blizzards. Fine grains of sand covering everything, including the linings of the lungs. A losing battle with locust, grasshoppers and drought that devoured any hope of a crop. Watching children lose weight and the light in their eyes go out. How did the parents in the 1930's cope with these circumstances? Sitting around their radio, they tuned into music that comforted their souls.

The Carter Family sang to all the families who huddled by their radio. "Will the Circle Be Unbroken?" was the question of their song. For those who had sons serving in the Conservation Corps, or had lost a family member to dust pneumonia, the hope of being reunited in this life or the next provided solace. The desire to leave the cares of this world resounded in Albert Brumley's down-home sound in "I'll Fly Away."

The Carter Family courtesy Wikipedia

As the agony of daily life left many with a feeling of total desperation, the words of Tommy Dorsey's song spoke for those seeking guidance. Tommy Dorsey experienced a great deal of suffering and loss in his life, so the lyrics he wrote came from deep in his soul. "Precious Lord, Take My Hand." Those in the Dust Bowl empathized with Dorsey's anguish, and made this song their prayer.

It is hard to imagine what a pastor of a church in the middle of devastating drought would pick to sing on a Sunday meeting. Maybe Fanny Crosby's visual, "He hideth my soul in the cleft of a rock that shadows a dry thirsty land" brought a vision of God's protection to those who felt vulnerable. For farmers, "There Shall Be Showers of Blessing" could be a hymn of hope when followed by "Bringing in the Sheaves." These discouraged farmers owned barren, lifeless land. But their souls experienced a spiritual drought. Relief for the soil or the soul needed cloudbursts, showers of blessing. Rain that could heal the land and revive the heart. For the pastors, bringing the right song to the congregation proved challenging.

Over the campfires of hobo camps or in the Hoovervilles, guitar players brought music to those riding the rail or enduring eviction. The songs of cowboys reminded these nomads of happier times. "The Red River Valley", "There Will Be Peace in the Valley", "You Are My Sunshine," or "Happy Trails to You" lent themselves to group singing and recalled the voices of the Sons of the Pioneers, Gene Autry or Roy Rogers. A musician among them, Woody Guthrie sang, "So Long, It's Been Good to Know You" and wrote "This Land Is Your Land." These iconic songs defined the plight of the men on the road and gave them a sense of community.

Woody Guthrie. March 1943. Credit: Al Aumuller, The Library of Congress, Prints & Photographs Division

In the late 1930's, when the Wizard of Oz exploded on the big screen, the hearts of the Americans in the Dust Bowl were searching for a place where everything was green and wishes could come true. They wanted the difficulties of life to be manageable. It was the mix of reality and a break from the harshness of reality that made Wizard of Oz successful. A place where the dreams that you dream come true. A place "Somewhere Over the Rainbow" where life would become normal again.

"Music washes from the soul the dust of everyday life." - Berthold Auerbach

"They were trailblazers for women in the military, for the Army Nurse Corps. They set the example for the rest of the services. Their story told the world…that women are tough, they can serve in combat and they can survive."
-Lt. Col. Nancy Cantrell, nurse and historian

Chapter Twenty-Two
A Quilt for the Angels of Bataan

Preparation from Life

The 99 Navy and Army nurses, known as "The Angels of Bataan", grew up in the Great Depression. Some of the women even endured the drought, dirt and deprivation of the Dust Bowl, eating Jack, biscuits and beans every meal of their lives. Others dined on dandelions or tumbleweeds. All lived in communities that knew how to hunker together to survive. That was how their parents made it through a decade of foraging for food, creatively fashioning tools, collecting fabric scraps to stitch into breathtaking quilts, and consoling one another at parlor room wakes. These young women witnessed the deep faith that underpinned the lives of the adults who raised them in desperate times. Like their parents, one day they would draw on that faith to endure uncharted challenges.

These young women were recruited by government workers who combed the small towns ravaged by poverty, seeking persons who knew how to face adversity. And wanted a ticket away from obscurity. With no military or survival training, the high school graduates signed up as Army or Navy Nurses. These medically trained inductees held the rank of second lieutenant and were universally addressed as "Miss."

Little did they know that the life skills learned in their youth would prepare them to face indescribable hardships as they battled for the lives of the GI's in the jungles of Bataan and in the Japanese prison camp in Manila.

Finding the Courage to Live

Right after Pearl Harbor, the Philippines fell under Japanese attack. The Army and Navy nurses were the first unit of American women to be sent into service so close to the front lines of battle. They quickly learned day by day to treat the wounded. Not in hospitals, but in outdoor clinics in the jungles of Bataan. Ruth Straub wrote in her journal about the first field hospital on Bataan. "It is jungle land and everyone lives under trees. Rows of beds snuggled under the trees with narrow winding paths between them and the night sky overhead."

National Archives photo

Laboring 24 hours a day for four months, the nurses cared for 6,000 patients while bombs whistled around them. In one day, January 16, 1942, the nurses aided the doctors in 187 major surgeries. The conditions defied medical standards. Lack of mosquito nets led to malaria and dengue fever among patients and staff. Swarms of flies contaminated the meager food and water supplies with dysentery and other parasites. Watching the women endure the same risks and illnesses as themselves, the soldiers fought with inspired courage. But in May, the US forces surrendered to the Japanese and the men were sent on the Bataan Death March. The nurses escaped under sniper fire, mines, and explosions to the Manila Tunnel where they tended the wounded. By then, they had earned their nickname, "the Angels of Bataan and Corregidor."

The nurses were taken prisoner, sent to Manila and held at a Japanese prison camp at Santo Tomas University with 4,000 prisoners. According to Nurse Mildred Manning, "We were scared and tired, but we kept working. We were under terrific strain, but we just did our job even when we were weak from not eating." During the imprisonment, the nurses treated fellow prisoners while suffering from beri-beri, dengue fever, malaria and malnutrition. "When your world is crumbling around you, you need this kind of structure," said Elizabeth Norman, associate professor of nursing at New York University.

The nurses assessed their fragile physical and mental reserves and knew they were dying after three years of prison life. They realized that the whole camp was on a death watch with a clock ticking. They made cynical jokes about it, but Lt. Palmer states, "None of these nurses ever expressed a fear to me about their own deaths, ever, either in battle or in the camp. It appeared to take more courage to live than to die."

Liberation

On February 3, 1944, the 1st Cavalry Division and 44th Tank Battalion burst through the prison gates. The nurses joined the prisoners as they cried and screamed, then sang, "God Bless America." When they left the prison on February 22, the women helped one another walk, stumble or limp to the trucks awaiting them. Each refused to be carried out. Ninety-nine nurses. One hundred per cent survival record. A feat unmatched to this day. A tribute to the years of childhood that taught them to hunker together, believe together, and make sure everyone walked out together.

The nurses returned to the States to resume their lives. They married, went back to military service, or worked. The government did not follow up on them, or understand the impact of their experiences on fertility, cancer, heart disease, chronic gastrointestinal problems, or dental work. The emotional and PTSD issues that resulted in relationship problems or suicide attempts never reached the government's desks. The nurses suffered in silence, another lesson they had learned as they grew up in the depths of the Great Depression.

The children of the 1930's came to terms with life at an early age, and stared fear in the face: just as their parents did on a daily basis. As young adults, they took on the perils of war with the same meddle as they had shown in their growing up years. Even as parents themselves, they coped with lingering memories and horrors, but rose to the challenge of building a better life for their children.

They have all become what we now know as *The Greatest Generation.*

"These, then, were the values installed in the four young Gates girls: hard work, education, perseverance, self-reliance, care-taking, and independence. With this as a foundation, it hardly seems surprising that one of them would eventually earn the title of hero." From the book, **Marcia Gates, Angel of Bataan** by Melissa Bowersock

"They were the largest group of women POW's in the history of our country. But there was so much going on- the events at Pearl Harbor, the war in Europe, that their story has been swallowed up." -Elizabeth Norman, author of **We Band of Angels**

National Archives Photo

"We weren't brave. We were just doing our job." - Lt. Helen Cassiani Nestor, **Angel of Bataan**

Chapter Twenty-Three
Sunbonnet Sue: Her Rise and Fall

My mother married in 1930, just as the Great Depression descended upon our country like locusts on a cornfield. Her life in the Dust Bowl area included a Hooverville, The Black Hand, midwife delivery of my older brother, and feed sack material for hand sewing. While my father worked six days a week, 12 hours a day digging irrigation ditches for Colorado beet farmers, Mom stitched together small scraps of flour bag muslin in calicos or plain colors. Her quilts still inspire admiration for their workmanship.

After my mother's death, a 12x12 inch block featuring Sunbonnet Sue lay in a closet with precisely folded scraps of fabric. Sewn with an embroidery stitch in black, Sue captured my imagination. Then I discovered the myriad of variations on the design. It fascinated me. Apparently, even my mother had succumbed to the allure of this popular applique pattern. During the Depression years, Sunbonnet Sue and her friend, Overall Sam, appeared on quilts, coloring books, tea towels, greeting cards, dishes and other decorative items. This 1930 pattern used up the pieces of material from sewing in a creative manner, which appealed to the frugal minded homemakers like my mother.

Quilt hand pieced from feed sacks by Cleo's mother, Ina Meiners

The basic design for Sunbonnet Sue can be traced to the late 1800's when British book editor, Kate Greenaway, introduced little girls in bonnets in the book **Under the Window** in 1878. But it was in the early 1900's that Sunbonnet Sue rose to folk image fame. In 1900 Bertha Corbett Melcher published a book, **The Sunbonnet Babies**, in which illustrator Eulalie Osgood Grover depicted young girls with their faces hidden by bonnets. Their books taught children how to read through the antics of Sunbonnet Sue, Fisherman Fred and Overall Sam. Teachers and parents enjoyed reading the books of this sweet, wholesome group of children to their own broods. Sue and the Gang caught on like caramel covering apples.

Applique templates from Ladies Art Patterns and McCall's Pattern Company depicted Sue in profile with an over-sized pinafore dress and large bonnet, like Melcher's illustrations in her book. The patterns were passed around in quilting clubs and embellished upon by each stitcher. Everyone interpreted Sunbonnet Sue's life from a unique vision. She flew kites, played with kittens, hung clothes on a line, carried books to school, and held hands with Overall Sam. During the poverty of the Great Depression, people yearned for reminders of happier days. The simple scenes of Sunbonnet Sue and Overall Sam brought a sense of sentimentality to the sewists enamored by the ever-present bonnet.

Perhaps the eventual lack of fascination of these faceless reflections of quilters' imagination should have been predicted. Too much sweetness and goo. In 1979, quilters in Lawrence, Kansas decided to take needles into their own hands. Calling themselves the "Seamsters Union Local #500", they created a twenty-block quilt. Each block depicted a method of death reflecting the culture of the 1970's. There are scenes of "Sunbonnet Sioux" shot with arrows, another with Sue being strangled by a sunflower. "Three Mile Island" Sue is surrounded by atoms. Even Jaws III swallowed up Sue. The quilt is now on display with the Michigan Quilt Project Museum.

Regardless of the antagonistic feelings of others, I still like Sunbonnet Sue and Overall Sam. When I wrote **Dust Between the Stitches,** the heroine created a family quilt using the feed sack scraps acquired from different sources in her Colorado Dust Bowl farm. Each chapter of the book is prefaced with a Sunbonnet Sue square that relates to the plot. The novel is a testimony to the stalwartness of those like my mother and father who faced adversity with quiet dignity.

One square of Sunbonnet Sue. A gift from my mother to me. It is part of my family's legacy of frugality and creativity despite difficult circumstances. Sunbonnet Sue represents my mother's strength of character.

Most important, that faceless bonnet is a visual representation of a generation of strong women.

Samples of illustrations from novel, **Dust Between the Stitches**

A Treasure

It's more than a coverlet,
More than a spread,
This beautiful quilt
That graces my bed.
It's laughter and sorrow,
It's pleasure and pain,
It's small bits and pieces
Of sunshine and rain.
It's a bright panorama
Of scraps of my life-
It's moments of glory,
It's moments of strife.
It's a story I cherish
Of days that have been,
It's a door I can open
To live them again. Yes, it's more than a cover
This much-treasured quilt,
Its parts pieced together
Of the life I have built.
Mildred Hatfield

Chapter Twenty-Four
Irish Patchwork: Piecing Frugality and Necessity

"When life gives you scraps, Make quilts" -anonymous

My mother's diary is filled with entries describing the latest finished quilt square that she hand-stitched in cabin camps, tents and a tiny wooden trailer while moving from job to job with my father during the 1930's Dust Bowl. As a young child, I lived with my Aunt Lois who spent her evenings embroidering pillow cases, or tea towels made from feed sacks. They turned fabric into works of art from their creative minds. These hard-working women of Scot-Irish heritage sewed from necessity and with frugality, traits handed down from generation to generation of Celtic ancestors to even me.

The history of Irish patchwork and needlework is one of women trying to not only survive, but to thrive in difficult circumstances. In the poverty-stricken villages, these stitchers gathered scraps of material around them and created patchwork quilts of amazing beauty. Each bit of fabric represented an opportunity to express their underestimated talents as artists. Most important, putting these pieces into cohesive designs provided color and a sense of luxury in households where a coat or a blanket covered a bed. Beauty in the home started with the desire for beauty in the feminine heart.

Needlework was second nature to most 19th century Irish girls who acquired quilt making skills from the English gentry who hired them as servants. They learned to wield a needle to make a living and to provide as a wife. Create, make do, and mend: the ultimate goal of these skills. Fabricating items of beauty from little or no supplies became the challenge as the women fashioned squares of log cabin, crazy, Irish chain, mosaic, block and applique for their homes.

Traditional Irish patchwork quilts comprised of only two layers: the top and the bottom stitched together in wave or chevron patterns. Most families cut up old clothing to make the patchwork top. Those who were too poor to use their clothing procured pieces from dressmakers, shop samples, factories and linen mills. Sometimes they gathered scraps from linen handkerchiefs, table cloths or pajama manufacturers for a touch of elegance. Shirt factories in Belfast produced many fabric scraps that were sold in bags according to weight. Workers stitched patchworks in their spare time and created a bit of cash flow for the family. These shirt patchwork quilts were named The Derry Quilts, The Shirt Quilts, and the Belfast Patchwork. The source and material labeled these comforters. The designs reflected the skill of the needle worker.

In the mountainous area of Ireland, sheep abounded. This allowed the possibility of a third, insulating layer of wool for the creators of patchworks. As a thrifty move, an old blanket or sheet could have been used to give extra weight and warmth to the primitive and rough looking creations. These rural areas boasted hand-woven fabrics like tweeds and suiting which contributed to their crazy quilts' functional appearance. A woman's desire for beauty gave way to necessity.

The potato famine in 1845-49 created an exodus from Ireland to America. The last night in Ireland was known as the American Wake, because no one expected to see those who emigrated ever again. Their few belongings were tied in a patchwork. Women stitched quilts on the long passage over. Roselind Shaw, an Irish quilt historian, states that "when the emigrants arrived on the beaches their quilts were washed and laid on the blocks to dry."[1]. In the United States, they discovered exciting patterns, and sent them back to their relatives to piece. By creating quilts with traditional Irish squares, and making the new ones at the same time as family across a cold sea, the fires of relationships still burned.

During the Second World War, the American Army was stationed in Northern Ireland. Although the Irish had access to plain white muslin feed bags that they used for backings, the women sought out the sacks from the American bakery in Crumlin, co. Antrim. The flour bags from the States were infused with color and designs that delighted the Irish quilt maker. A bit of beauty in the midst of need.

Times changed. The Irish gave in to the materialistic ways of the world, and traded in their old bedding for the look of candlewick and fine linens. The older generation viewed the patchwork quilts as reminders of hard times when they cut up their clothes for bedding. Ridding themselves of the past provided avenues for beauty and hope in the futures of these Irish immigrants.

When I go into thrift shops or walk through garage sales, the quilts call my name from under stacks of tossed items. Sometimes the fabric quality is good, but many times it is apparent that the material is losing its weave. I like to imagine the woman who took the time to stitch the pieces together, and consider the pattern and fabrics she chose. Were any of the materials recycled? A patchwork is a snapshot into a woman's life, heart and mind. A testimony of her necessity and frugality. A hint of her creativity and love of beauty.

Touching the fabrics of a quilt reminds me of my mother, my aunt, my heritage. It reminds me of home.

May the raindrops fall lightly on your brow.
May the soft winds freshen your spirit.
May the sunshine brighten your heart
May the burdens of the day rest lightly upon you.
And may God enfold you in the patchwork of His love.

Irish Blessing

Chapter Twenty-Five
Seminole Patchwork Skirts: A Quilting Philosophy

"Whenever you are creating beauty around you, you are restoring your own soul." – Alice Walker

Life on the Florida reservation brought challenges to the women who faced the hardships of Everglade living. Resources were few. The threat of depression hung like the billowy clouds overhead. In the Seminole Indian homes called chickees, the women of the early 1900's hunkered in and found a philosophy of life to transcend their harsh circumstances. As the adage says, "When life gives you scraps, make quilts." In the case of the Seminole tribe, the women did not sew bed coverings. These stitchers designed quilted clothing. They created beauty from fabric with an underlying philosophy of life centered on three core values: tribal pride, a belief in life, and creative expression.

Binding Cultural Heritage

The Seminole Indian women developed a form of patchwork that differed from the traditional piecework of the missionaries who taught them how to join fabrics. Their wearable art also differed from the Irish patchwork stitched by survivors of the potato famine.

National Archives

The Seminole patchwork skirts stood in sharp contrast to the scrappy quilt work of the women of the Dust Bowl who used feed bags for their work. In the shelter of their chickees, the Indian women created cloth that reflected a commitment to sustainability, functionality and a personal narrative. Early designs were bars of alternating colors or a saw-tooth design. These bands of designs were sewn together to form the skirt or shirt's fabric. Together, the women developed a highly visible art form distinguished by bright mosaic-like patterns that reflected their tribal pride and positive attitudes.

Like the other quilters of the early 1900's, frugality reigned. The ends of fabric bolts became the sought-after scrap needed for these one-of –a-kind creations. The narrow layers of cloth produced a technique that made the Seminole tribe the "grandmother of strip piecing". But their wearable art was not just about making something pretty. It represented the strength of people living under oppressive circumstances. With bobbins whirring, these women proved the words of Pablo Picasso: "Art washes away from the soul the dust of everyday life."

Pulling the Common Thread

In every heart beats the desire to feel that life is worthwhile. Henry Moore expressed this core value best when he stated, "To be an artist is to believe in life." As the Seminole women cut and sewed row after row of intricately multicolored bands in border or frieze patterns, they found music for the soul in the rhythm of the needles. Quilting became a way to reduce anxiety over the future, to combat depression, and to improve their creative thinking. Another visual artist, Georgia O'Keefe, explains how the Seminole women must have felt as they sewed on their treadle machines. "I have found that I could say things with color and shapes that I couldn't say any other way. Things that I had not words for." With each stitch, beauty emerged, and the resolve of the quilter to enter joyously into life grew deeper.

Art is the journey of the free soul.

National Archives

Expanding on Patterns

The unique patchwork of the Seminole tribe is not your Grandmother's traditional piecework. The women took the basic principles quilting, added frugality, and introduced a legacy of originality. The mathematical symmetry of design in the skirts is unparalleled and difficult to repeat. The ability to stitch together narrow strips of material became the tribe's signature look. As true artists the quilters pushed past their own technical and aesthetic knowledge and created new techniques for the well -worn predictable patterns. When the sewing machine became the standard tool in every 1920 chickee, the ability to make wearable art in the form of patchwork skirts for the women, and striped shirts for men, dominated the tribe.

Soon, the women developed a market for their clothing line to the tourist trade in the Everglades. This created a commercial market for their uniquely designed patchwork items. As the treasured sewing techniques are handed down from one generation to the next, Seminole patchwork has become an important means of income as well as Tribal and creative pride. "If you want to be original, be ready to be copied," warns Coco Chanel.

The patchwork skirts of the Seminole Indians represent the core values of cultural identity, love of life and development of original fabric expression. The work of the women's hands demonstrates that whatever a person believes on the inside is manifest on the outside. In the case of these quilters, one admires the view of colorful, intricate patterns on fabric. The outward reflection from an inward philosophy of abiding optimism.

Beautiful.

"A personal style is like handwriting- it happens as the by-product of our own way of seeing things, enriched by the experiences of everything around us." – M.Vignelli

Conclusion

"If you would like to have your heart broken, just come out here. This is the dust-storm country. It is the saddest land I have ever seen."

Ernie Pyle, journalist, 1936

The folks in the Dust Bowl lived through tough times. Black blizzards, dust pneumonia, bank foreclosure, drought, rabbit plagues, locusts, and lack of water crowded into everyday life. Rumors of those who gave up hope encroached upon the faith of the ones who clung onto life like a dried-out thread. Yet every morning that the sun shone meant one more day of survival in an environment where snakes slithered to escape the heat. Days turned into weeks, which turned into years, and then a decade before the break that the homesteaders needed.

Our generation stands on the shoulders of those who faced fear itself on a daily basis. By doing so, the people of the Dust Bowl learned to extend compassion, an encouraging word, or a glass of water to the thirsty. Their children grew up to be creative, determined, independent and frugal. They had watched their parents dig deep into the wells of their faith for the strength to face each new day of challenges. Many families gave from their poverty to those who had nothing at all. The tough times created a solid foundation on which to build a life without frills. A generation that moved through a world war, married, raised children, volunteered for community organizations, and provided a legacy of integrity.

The tough times of the Dust Bowl produced the Greatest Generation.

"Although the world is full of suffering, it is also full of the overcoming of it."

Helen Keller

Photo Credits and Links

Chapter One
Main photo credit: https://morguefile.com/p/51587
http://cleolampos.com/the-dust-bowl-how-did-it-happen

Chapter Two
Main photo credit: https://morguefile.com/p/51587
http://cleolampos.com/henry-finnell-the-dust-storms-answer-to-if-it-rain

Chapter Three
http://cleolampos.com/hugh-hammond-bennett-the-dust-bowls-advocate

Chapter Four
Main photo: National Archives
http://cleolampos.com/feed-sacks-the-fabric-of-the-dust-bowl

Chapter Five
Main photo and men on train photos courtesy of Partridge, Rondal, 1917-, Photographer (NARA record: 8464464) - U.S. National Archives and Records Administration
http://cleolampos.com/hobos-the-dust-bowlss-rail-riders

Chapter Six
Main photo by Dorthea Lange for the WPA.
https://commons.wikimedia.org/wiki/File:Lange-MigrantMother02.jpg
http://cleolampos.com/hoovervilles-the-cities-of-the-great-depression

Chapter Seven
http://cleolampos.com/dust-pneumonia-when-breathing-is-deadly

Chapter Eight
http://cleolampos.com/the-dust-bowl-diet-eating-in-a-drought
Main photo credit: *National Archives*

Chapter Nine
Main photo: National Archives
http://cleolampos.com/leo-hart-the-school-for-dust-bowl-refugees

Chapter Ten
Main photo: Photo of eight boys on bench by Dorothea Lange
http://cleolampos.com/5-lessons-for-todays-teachers-from-weedpatch-camp-school

Chapter Eleven
http://cleolampos.com/radio-the-voices-from-the-air

Chapter Twelve
http://cleolampos.com/piecing-a-legacy-a-1930-quilt-story

Chapter Thirteen
Main photo: National Archives
http://cleolampos.com/a-picture-worth-thousands-of-words-the-dust-bowl-by-ken-burns

Chapter Fourteen
Main photo: https://morguefile.com/creative/Alvimann
http://cleolampos.com/bon-appetite-depression-style

Chapter Fifteen
Main photo: National Archives
http://cleolampos.com/feeding-the-mind-pack-horse-library-project

Chapter Sixteen
http://cleolampos.com/dust-bowl-photojournalists

Chapter Seventeen
Main photo: National Archives
http://cleolampos.com/dust-bowl-from-ccc-to-greatest-generation

Chapter Eighteen
Main photo: http://www.freedigitalphotos.net/images/Fruit_g104-Three_Oranges_On_White_Background_p36302.html
http://cleolampos.com/coloring-christmas-orange-celebrating-in-the-great-depression

Chapter Nineteen
Main photo: htttps://morguefile.com/p/793837
Photo credit: https://morguefile.com/p/43137
http://cleolampos.com/stitches-in-time

Chapter Twenty
http://cleolampos.com/irish-immigration-and-the-orphan-trains-changed-the-direction-of-my-life
Main photo: National Archives

Chapter Twenty-One
Main photo credit: "Migrant family from Arkansas playing hill-billy songs," Farm Security Administration emergency migrant camp, photo by Dorothea Lange, February 1939
http://cleolampos.com/singing-in-hard-times

Chapter Twenty-Two
http://cleolampos.com/a-quilt-for-the-angels-of-bataan

Chapter Twenty-Three
http://cleolampos.com/sunbonnet-sue-her-rise-and-fall

Chapter Twenty-Four
Main photo: http://www.freedigitalphotos.net/images/countryside-on-dingle-peninsula-photo-p341997
http://cleolampos.com/irish-patchwork-piecing-frugality-and-necessity

Chapter Twenty-Five
http://cleolampos.com/seminole-patchwork-skirts-a-quilting-philosophy

ABOUT THE AUTHOR

Born in Greeley, Colorado, Cleo Lampos grew up in three states: Colorado, Iowa and Wisconsin. She attended nine schools before graduating from Fort Atkinson High School in Wisconsin. Lampos earned a Bachelor's Degree in Elementary Education from the University of Wisconsin-Whitewater. Her minor was library science. Lampos taught fourth grade and special education in the public schools for 26 years in Oak Lawn- Hometown District 123 and Cook County District 130. She is listed in **Who's Who in Among American Teachers.**

Lampos was married with three children when she earned her Master's Degree in Special Education from St. Xavier University. She was listed in **Who's Who in American Universities**. During this time, she began writing articles for teacher trade magazines and religious publications. Since then, she has authored seven books, many more articles, and writes a weekly blog. Lampos is a frequent speaker of historical topics at McHenry Community College, Trinity College, Harper College, and at the Renaissance Academy of St. Xavier University. In her free time, Lampos has been a member in a quilting group, her local church, the Oak Lawn writer's club, and has volunteered at the Oak Lawn Community Garden.

During the summer of 2017, Lampos and her husband took a class through the Illinois Agricultural Extension Service and are now Master Urban Farmers. Their extensive home garden and shelves of canned produce are proof of their green thumbs. Eleven grandchildren and three adult children with spouses keep Lampos busy. FOR MORE INFO VISIT: WWW.CLEOLAMPOS.COM

Check out Cleo's Other Books!

Rescuing Children: Teachers, Social Workers, Nuns and Missionaries Who Stepped in the Shadows to Rescue Waifs

Rescuing Children explores the compelling work of Irean Sendler and the Warsaw Ghetto, Jane Addams and the Hull House, Dr. Thomas Barnardo and his work with orphanages, Gladys Aylward and China's orphans, Amy Carmicheal and India's Temple children, Sister Irene and Charles Loring Brace and their orphan trains, and Bertha Bracey and the Kindertransport. Each of these individuals faced the social issues of their time head-on...Issues that mirror many modern challenges. From the past, we learn to deal with the present and prepare for the future.

Available on Amazon!

Dust Between the Stitches

Addy Meyer wants to teach children in a one room school house in Colorado during the 1930's Dust Bowl. Black Blizzards, the Board of Education, and bank president overwhelm her. Addy falls in love with the orphans her grandfather adopted, and her students, but vows to guard her heart against Jess Dettmann, who has a suspicious past. Foreclosure on grandpa's homestead threatens the security of all of them. Creating a quilt from Grandma's stash pile serves as a way for Addy to cope, but eventually leads to help and justice for her family. Despair, dust and drought weave through the Great Depression and Dust Bowl producing a fabric on which vivid threads of hope appear. Will Addy save the farm, her job, and her heart on the Colorado ranch?

Available on **Amazon**!

Teaching Diamonds in the TOUGH: A Teacher's Devotional

Finding the potential in students is challenging regardless of the setting, be it public school, private school, church clubs, youth groups, or Sunday school. Through illustrative episodes drawn from her teaching experiences, this devotional encourages teachers to work and pray past the struggles and heartbreaks teachers face.

With Scripture, quotes, and a suggested action plan, this devotional will help teachers give affection, attention, and guidance to those students considered too tough to learn. See beyond the rough exteriors of a student's attitude and behavior to their inner needs. No student is ever lost or too tough to teach when they are loved. Learn how to change hearts and minds with God's help.

Available on Amazon!

A Mother's Song: A Story of the Orphan Train

In 1890, Deirdre O'Sullivan lives in Five Points, New York City with her husband, son and four-year-old, Ava Rose. Pregnant with their third child, Deirdre works as a washerwoman at the hotel's laundry. If Sean works at all, he drinks his paycheck at the pub. When he is killed in an accident at work, Deirdre is devastated. She gives birth to another son, but cannot work at the laundry. The oldest son lives on the street as a newsie. Rather than let Ava Rose and her baby brother starve to death with her, she signs for them to be put on an orphan train. This orphan train takes these youngsters to Nebraska to Claudine, who has suffered multiple miscarriages. Will the adoption provide the safety and opportunity that Deirdre hopes? This researched story of two mothers and the child who loves both is heart wrenching. It is a poignant tale of hope and courage against unfathomable odds for a better life free from prejudice and poverty. Available on Amazon!

Second Chances

Zoey Pappas grew up in a one-stoplight town. Now she's landed her dream job as the fifth grade teacher at the urban Diamond Projects School, but can she handle it? Her family laid odds that she won't. Zoey know s her cows, but she's never dealt with students from drug-infested, crime-ridden communities. Her Greek family wants her to work in the family restaurant and earn her M.R.S. degree. Zoey wants to prove herself, but she has met a muscled Irish cop who has been assigned to work with her as the Drug Awareness officer. He's too efficient, to cocky, and too... handsome.

Ever since Officer Gavien Corrigan pulled Zoey's car over on her first day of school for driving on a one way street in a neighborhood known for violence, he's been captivated by her. Thoughts of the new teacher crowd in with the family responsibilities that overshadow his life. His bullet proof vest is lighter than the secret blame he carries on his shoulders. He believes that God is in control of lives, but sometimes wonders if God has forgotten him.

As the two are thrust together in the concrete jungle where everyone needs second chances, will Zoey and Gavin find their own second chances...together?

Zoey learns of unconditional love as she becomes friends with Carole Milner and her husband who is wheelchair bound with multiple sclerosis. As she watches the couple cope with MS, Zoey desires to fall in love like them. Multiple sclerosis does not define their relationship, love does.

A deaf student is mainstreamed into Zoey's class, so she enters the world of the deaf and hard of hearing. It moves Zoey to deeper compassion for the parents and foster parents in her classroom.

Anyone who has been a teacher, or loves children will enjoy this romance that brings the country girl into the urban scene. A fresh look at chaplains working in jail ministry, drug rehab and foster care are included in this novel set in the inner city. The influence of Greek immigrant ideas are also explored. Will Zoey make it in the big city?

Available on **Amazon**!

Miss Bee and the Do Bees: An Urban Teacher Romance

Roni Bagedonas faces challenges as a special education teacher with an autistic student and an emotionally disturbed pupil in her classroom of six special needs children. Roni's private issues with body image are pressed by the former beauty queen who is now her aide. Joe Malinkavich is back from Afghanistan where he served as a medic. Dealing with PTSD, Joe is an emergency responder for the fire department. Both Roni and Joe want a relationship, but find obstacles. When they are confronted with the issues of life in a visit at a VA Hospital, they set new priorities. This book explores the issues of PTSD, body image, challenges of urban education, autistic children, foster care and forgiveness. Written as a light romance, the novel also has an inspirational focus that will feed the soul as well as the mind. The unique challenges of Chicago are highlighted in the book that includes realistic events in an inner-city school setting. Anyone who enjoyed Stand and Deliver, A Tree Grows in Brooklyn, My Posse Don't Do Homework, or Tisha will appreciate this book.

Available on **Amazon**!

Cultivating Wildflowers: An Urban Teacher Romance

Summer isn't looking good for Alana Alcott, an urban teacher of gifted students. She's been court ordered to teach summer school with Outward Bound instructor Mike Reynolds. Their students? Five unruly foster kids whose stories of abandonment mirror Alana's own childhood more than she wants to admit.

Mike, in particular, initially chafes on Alana's nerves. She sees him as an overgrown Boy Scout, promoting a nature-to-nurture philosophy that may or may not help their troubled students. And troubled they certainly are, with problems ranging from behavioral issues to a looming gang recruitment.

As Mike and Alana struggle to help their young charges connect with nature in the bleak concrete landscape of the projects, the two teachers find themselves increasingly attracted to each other. The demands of their students, however, interrupt their blossoming romance at every turn. Alana, meanwhile, finds herself forced to confront her own past—and the mother who abandoned her.

Over the course of one short summer, seven lives will change, for good or ill. If Mike and Alana can help it, their students will find hope and direction. Doing so, however, may mean putting their own happiness on hold—or sacrificing it forever.

Available on **Amazon**!

GRANDPA'S REMEMBERING BOOK

Available on Amazon!

Made in the USA
Lexington, KY
16 December 2017